FLAGSHIP HISTORYMAKERS

STALIN

JOHN PHILIP

Collins

An imprint of HarperCollins*Publishers*

Dedication
For Mary, Roisín, Sinéad and Aisling.

Published by HarperCollins*Publishers* Ltd
77–85 Fulham Palace Road
London
W6 8JB

Browse the complete Collins catalogue at
www.collinseducation.com

© HarperCollins*Publishers* Ltd 2004
First published 2004

ISBN 0 00 717361 X

John Philip asserts the moral right to be identified
as the author of this work.

British Library Cataloguing in Publication Data. A
catalogue record for this book is available from the
British Library.

Series commissioned by Graham Bradbury
Project management by Will Chuter
Edited by Marie Insall
Book and cover design by Derek Lee
Map artwork by Richard Morris
Picture research by Celia Dearing
Production by Sarah Robinson
Printed and bound by Martins, Berwick upon Tweed

ACKNOWLEDGEMENTS

The Publishers would like to thank the following
for permission to reproduce extracts from their
books:

Harcourt Education for extracts from *Stalinist
Russia* by Steven Phillips (2000). Weidenfeld &
Nicholson for extracts from *Stalin, Man of History*,
by Ian Grey (1979).

The Publishers would like to thank the following
for permission to reproduce pictures on these pages
T=Top, B=Bottom, L=Left, R=Right, C=Centre

David King Collection 8, 9T&B, 22T&C&B, 23T&B,
25, 27, 52, 53, 57L&R; © Getty Images/Hulton
Archive 7, 19, 31, 32, 36L&R, 39T&B, 48;
Rendezvous, cartoon by David Low, Evening
Standard 20/9/1939/Centre for the Study of
Cartoons and Caricature, University of Kent 33.

Cover picture: © Bettmann/Corbis

Every effort has been made to contact the holders
of copyright material, but if any have been
inadvertently overlooked the Publishers will be
pleased to make the necessary arrangements at the
first opportunity.

You might also like to visit
www.harpercollins.co.uk
The book lovers' website

Contents

Why do historians differ?

HE purpose of the Flagship Historymakers series is to explore the main debates surrounding a number of key individuals in British, European and American History.

Each book begins with a chronology of the significant events in the life of the particular individual, and an outline of the person's career. The book then examines in greater detail three of the most important and controversial issues in the life of the individual – issues which continue to attract differing views from historians, and which feature prominently in examination syllabuses in A-level History and beyond.

Each of these issue sections provides students with an overview of the main arguments put forward by historians. By posing key questions, these sections aim to help students to think through the areas of debate and to form their own judgements on the evidence. It is important, therefore, for students to understand why historians differ in their views on past events and, in particular, on the role of individuals in past events.

The study of history is an ongoing debate about events in the past. Although factual evidence is the essential ingredient of history, it is the *interpretation* of factual evidence that forms the basis for historical debate. The study of how and why historians differ in their various interpretations is termed 'historiography'.

Historical debate can occur for a wide variety of reasons.

Insufficient evidence

In some cases there is insufficient evidence to provide a definitive conclusion. In attempting to 'fill the gaps' where factual evidence is unavailable, historians use their professional judgement to make 'informed comments' about the past.

New evidence

As new evidence comes to light, an historian today may have more information on which to base judgements than historians in the past. For instance, following the denunciation of Stalin in 1956, new documentary evidence within the USSR became available to historians. More importantly, the fall of the USSR in 1991 allowed Russian archival material to become more accessible to western historians. In addition, Russian historians have become freer to analyse and comment on their own national archives.

A 'philosophy' of history?

Many historians have a specific view of history that will affect the way they make their historical judgements. For instance, Marxist historians – who take their view from the writings of Karl Marx, the founder of modern socialism – believe that society has always been made up of competing economic and social classes. They also place considerable importance on economic reasons behind human decision-making. Therefore, a Marxist historian looking at an historical issue may take a completely different viewpoint to a non-Marxist historian.

The role of the individual

Some historians have seen past history as being largely moulded by the acts of specific individuals. Hitler, Mussolini and Stalin are seen as individuals whose personality and beliefs changed the course of twentieth-century European history. Other historians have tended to play down the role of the individuals; instead, they highlight the importance of more general social, economic and political change. Rather than seeing Joseph Stalin as an individual who changed the course of political history, these historians tend to see him as representing the views of post-Lenin communists within the USSR. If Stalin had not existed another leader would have taken his place.

Placing different emphasis on the same historical evidence

Even if historians do not possess different philosophies of history or place different emphasis on the role of the individual, it is still possible for them to disagree in one very important way. This is that they may place different emphases on aspects of the same factual evidence. As a result, History should be seen as a subject that encourages debate about the past, based on historical evidence.

Historians will always differ

Historical debate is, in its nature, continuous. What today may be an accepted view about a past event may well change in the future, as the debate continues.

Timeline: Stalin's life

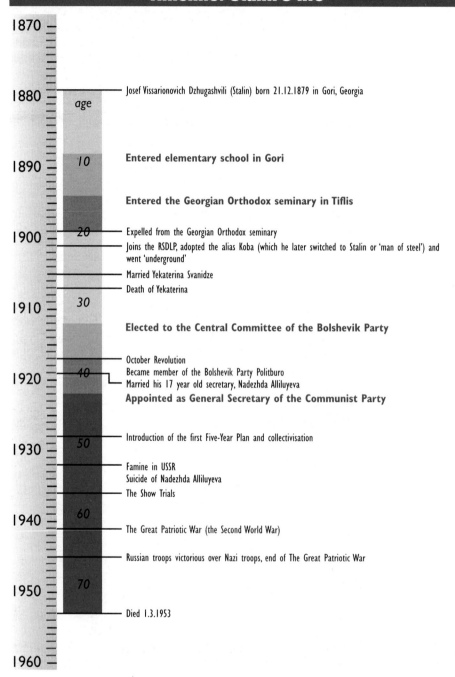

1870

1880 — age — Josef Vissarionovich Dzhugashvili (Stalin) born 21.12.1879 in Gori, Georgia

1890 — 10 — **Entered elementary school in Gori**

Entered the Georgian Orthodox seminary in Tiflis

1900 — 20 — Expelled from the Georgian Orthodox seminary
— Joins the RSDLP, adopted the alias Koba (which he later switched to Stalin or 'man of steel') and went 'underground'
— Married Yekaterina Svanidze
— Death of Yekaterina

1910 — 30

Elected to the Central Committee of the Bolshevik Party

— October Revolution
1920 — 40 — Became member of the Bolshevik Party Politburo
— Married his 17 year old secretary, Nadezhda Alliluyeva
Appointed as General Secretary of the Communist Party

— Introduction of the first Five-Year Plan and collectivisation

1930 — 50
— Famine in USSR
Suicide of Nadezhda Alliluyeva
— The Show Trials

1940 — 60
— The Great Patriotic War (the Second World War)

— Russian troops victorious over Nazi troops, end of The Great Patriotic War

1950 — 70

— Died 1.3.1953

1960

Stalin addressing the soviet at the height of his leadership.

Stalin: a brief biography

How did Stalin make history?

Joseph Stalin (1879–1953) came to personify the USSR, which he led from the late 1920s until his death, and perhaps the entire Communist system. Commonly regarded as one of the ogres of twentieth-century history, he is popularly identified with **show trials**, **purges** and executions. There are many debates concerning Stalin's role within Russian history. On the one hand, his actions from 1944 onwards are viewed as plunging Europe, and then the world, into the **Cold War**. Yet he is also regarded as the man who drove his country down the path of industrialisation at an astonishing rate in the 1930s, during a decade of world depression. It is widely accepted that it is only because of Stalin and his policies that the USSR managed to withstand the Nazi invasion of 1941. His takeover of much of Eastern Europe from 1945 has also been seen as a successful attempt to protect the USSR from further attack and to spread communism.

Early life and influences

Stalin's early life in Georgia was spent in constant poverty. His parents were both born as **serfs**. His father was a drunken and brutal shoemaker who died when Stalin was eleven. His highly religious mother worked hard as a servant, a seamstress and washer-woman. When he was eight she gained him a place in the local, and strictly Christian, elementary school, where he learned to speak **Russian**. By the time he left, aged 14, Stalin was top of his class and had won a free scholarship to the seminary for priests in the state capital, Tiflis. While at the seminary, his **revolutionary** tendencies began to surface. He controversially began preaching Marxism rather than Orthodox Christianity.

At the same time, in 1894, **Nicholas II** became Tsar. Opposition

Show trial: a highly publicised trial in which the confession is faked and usually a false verdict given.

Purges: the removal of opponents.

Cold War: a conflict of military tension and political hostility between the USA and the USSR and their respective allies from the end of WWII until the collapse of the USSR in 1991.

Serf: a labourer who belonged to the landowner and could be bought and sold as a slave.

Russian: the reign of Tsar Alexander III (1881–1894) saw an intensification of a process known as Russification. This was intended to make the minority nations of the empire, like Georgia, speak and think like Russians.

Revolutionary: a person who supports drastic ideas which oppose those of a political system or society.

Tsar Nicholas II (1894–1917) the last Tsar (emperor) of the Romanov dynasty that had ruled the Russian Empire from 1613. The Tsars ruled as autocrats (monarchs with absolute power) and Nicholas's reign was epitomised by force and repression. He and his family were executed by the communists in 1918 during the Russian Civil War (1918–20).

Karl Marx (1818–1883) a German political philosopher and founding father of Marxism (Communism). Marx believed that history was a series of class struggles which would inevitably lead to the triumph of the proletariat (working-class).

RSDLP: the Russian Social Democratic Worker's Party, the formal name of the Russian Communist Party.

Bolsheviks and **Mensheviks**: the two emergent factions of the RSDLP caused by polarised views concerning party organisation and revolutionary violence. The Mensheviks favoured a loose-knit form of party organisation with a more democratic leadership, while the Bolsheviks supported the political system introduced by Lenin after the Russian Revolution in 1917.

spiralled during his reign, given a fresh impetus by the introduction of the teachings of **Karl Marx** into Russia. During this time the young Stalin joined a secret Georgian group called Messame Dassy. While some members supported Georgian independence from Russia, others, including Stalin, were emerging as Socialist Revolutionaries. In 1899, aged 19, Stalin was expelled from the Tiflis Seminary for his attempts to convert fellow students to Marxism.

By 1900, Stalin had become a revolutionary. In 1901, aged 21, he joined the **RSDLP** while most of the key leaders were in exile in London. Unlike most members at the time, Stalin was working class. His willingness to work hard within Russia as a revolutionary agitator against his own family roots and religion illustrates his ruthless nature. By 1902 he had gone underground in an unsuccessful attempt to conceal his identity from the authorities. Caught by the Tsarist police in 1903, Stalin was exiled to a Siberian labour camp for his political activities. Meanwhile, in London, the exiled leaders of the Social Democrats were splitting their party into the **Bolsheviks** and **Mensheviks**. Stalin became a Bolshevik, favouring the use of revolutionary violence. In 1905 he met **Lenin**, leader of the Bolsheviks, for the first time. This year also saw his marriage to Yekaterina Svanidze. The following year he spoke at the Fourth Party Congress in Stockholm. A repetitive cycle of imprisonment, exile and escape toughened Stalin during the next eleven years. On a personal level, the death of his wife in 1907 hardened his heart. After her funeral Stalin stated: 'She is dead and with her have died my last warm feelings for human beings'. These events greatly affected the 28 year-old Stalin, and marked the beginning of a more ruthless and determined phase in his life.

In a brief period of freedom in 1912 Stalin became editor of *Pravda*, the official Bolshevik newspaper. Earlier that year, while still in exile, he was elected in his absence to the Central Committee of the Bolshevik Party. Arrested again in 1913, he was exiled to Northern Siberia. After the abdication of Nicholas II in

Lenin (1870–1924): Vladimir Ilich Lenin. A radical in his early life, Lenin distinguished himself as a prolific writer and publicist explaining Marxist theory and conveying his views for Russia's socialism. In 1903 he provoked a split in the Russian Social Democratic Labour Party, between the Bolsheviks and Mensheviks. The next few years of his life were spent in exile until 1917, after the February Revolution. He urged for the seizure of power by the working classes, and led the Bolshevik revolution in October to become the head of the first Soviet government.

Provisional Government: temporary government set up by former members of Nicholas II's parliament after his abdication.

Petrograd: Russia's second capital (after Moscow), re-named Petrograd during the First World War and became Leningrad in honour of Lenin after his death in 1924. Reverted to St Petersburg in the early 1990s, following the collapse of the USSR.

Petrograd Soviet: one of the soviets, or workers' councils which emerged during the failed Revolution of 1905 and rivalled the Provisional Government. It was dominated by the Mensheviks until September 1917 when the Bolsheviks secured a majority.

October Revolution: the armed takeover by the Bolsheviks, led by Lenin, of the provisional government in 1917.

Civil War (1918–20): an attempted counter-revolution by the Whites: a loose coalition of opponents including landowners, those who wanted a return to a democracy and some socialists and former WWI allies. The Bolsheviks, known as the Reds, defeated them.

February 1917, the newly established **Provisional Government** released the Tsar's political prisoners, and Stalin was able to return to **Petrograd**. He became editor of *Pravda* again, and gained a seat on the Politburo, the Executive Committee of the **Petrograd Soviet**. While Lenin was in exile, Stalin supported the continuation of Russia's involvement in the First World War. However, upon Lenin's return in April, Stalin followed 'Lenin's line' on all policy, without playing any major role in the events that led to the Bolshevik seizure of power in October. In his personal life, in 1919, Stalin married his young secretary, Nadezha.

The path to power

After the **October Revolution** the Communist Party had difficulty governing Russia. Between 1918 and 1921 the country was at **Civil War**. From 1921, the primary task was to deal with the huge problems of economic collapse, poverty and famine that were facing the new state.

Although Stalin was by no means regarded as one of the Communist Party's leading lights, between 1917 and 1922 he quietly increased his power. The critical moment was his appointment as General Secretary of the Communist Party in 1922. This gave him almost unlimited administrative authority. Various incidents led Lenin to question the wisdom of this appointment, but other leading communists were more concerned about preventing Trotsky's succession.

By late 1922, Lenin, who had been shot in 1918, was seriously unwell. Stalin formed a **Triumvirate** with two other Bolshevik members to govern together in the event of Lenin's death. Lenin suffered a further stroke in March 1923 and died in January 1924.

Leader of the USSR

In 1928–9 Stalin introduced the twin policies of **'collectivisation'** and the **'Five-Year Plans'** that were aimed at the transformation of the USSR both in terms of agriculture and industry. Despite significant industrial advances, Stalin's economic policies led to a famine in 1932–3 that was hidden from the world, and provoked

Triumvirate: a group of three people sharing power. The Triumvirate worked towards a joint succession to Lenin, and to prevent Trotsky from becoming too powerful.

'Collectivisation': neighbouring peasants were forced to merge their lands into 'collective farms' called *Kolkhozee*. This was in line with the Marxist principle of state ownership of the means of production.

'Five-Year Plans': a government plan implemented for economic development involving rapid industrialisation and the collectivisation of agriculture.

Understanding Stalin

- **Responsible for many radical changes to the USSR**, most notably through the Five-Year Plans.

- **Fond of a simple life**, either in the Kremlin or at his dacha (country house); often sitting up drinking and talking half the night with his most trusted associates.

- **Very determined in his pursuit of goals**, for example his pursuit of power; considered by some as cunning in his scheming.

- **A pragmatic man** who was capable of switching policies or making alliances for practical reasons rather than for principles.

- **A paranoid man**, he appears to have seen enemies everywhere, **ruthless** in his determination to crush them and **extremely cruel**.

- **Incapable of feeling pity**, possibly relating to the death of his first wife.

- **In many ways an insecure man**, denying his Georgian roots yet never really a Russian.

- **A cold man** who could reject his own mother, drive his second wife to suicide and deny to the Germans during the Second World War that one of their captured prisoners of war was his eldest son, Yakov.

- **A vengeful man** who would seek revenge either against a person or a people if he felt the urge.

- **Coarse and rude** in his personal attacks on people.

- **Boastful and arrogant**, he believed he had talents in all areas – for example military strategy – where the evidence does not always support his conclusions.

- **Determined to be adored**, he foisted the 'cult of his personality' on the Russian public, fostering an image of almost superhuman status.

'A sickly old man, unpredictable, dangerous, lied to by terrified subordinates and raging ... against failure and mortality'.
Chris Ward

the suicide of his second wife. However, Stalin saw industrial development as essential for the safety of the USSR, the only communist state in a hostile capitalist world.

The 1930s saw Stalin consolidating his power and creating a terror state. The old Bolsheviks and rivals from the 1920s were placed on show trial and executed. In 1940, the murder of Trotsky marked the elimination of the last of Stalin's rivals.

By August 1939, with the world once more on the brink of war, Stalin attempted to isolate the USSR from the coming conflict by signing the **Nazi-Soviet Pact** with Hitler's Germany. This proved to be a short-lived respite. In June 1941 Hitler invaded the USSR. For the next four years the Soviet people suffered dreadfully as a result of the Nazi invasion. However, a combination of factors led to the turning of the tide. By 1944 the German Armies were being driven back through Eastern Europe by the **Red Army**. In the summer of 1944 the USSR's wartime allies, the USA and Britain, had launched a second front in France. By 1945 Soviet troops were in Berlin, triumphing over Nazism.

The Grand Alliance between the USA, Britain and the USSR was always an unlikely relationship between two capitalist democracies and a communist dictatorship. Strains that were already evident during the war, swiftly deepened from 1945. This led to the Cold War, which effectively dominated the last eight years of Stalin's life. Stalin was effectively in control of most of Eastern Europe by 1948. Until 1949 the main focus of the Cold War was in Europe, but the fall of China to communism in 1949, and the start of the **Korean War** in 1950, saw the focus switch towards Asia in Stalin's final years.

After the Second World War Stalin introduced a fourth Five-Year. This was aimed at rebuilding Soviet industry following the destruction of war. By 1950, Soviet industry was stronger than before the Second World War – a remarkable achievement. Collectivisation had virtually collapsed during the war but was reintroduced vigorously after 1945. In terms of his personal dictatorship, Stalin effectively abandoned any pretence that policies were a matter for debate. Neither the Politburo nor the Central Committee met between 1947 and 1952. The purges and terror were intensified. There were almost 2.5 million prisoners in the labour camps at the time of Stalin's death.

On 1 March 1953, aged 74, Stalin collapsed in his bedroom. When his body was found there was some delay in seeking medical assistance, possibly in case he recovered and blamed those who found him for his condition. He was declared dead on 5 March 1953.

Nazi-Soviet Pact (1939): a treaty signed in Moscow on behalf of Germany and the USSR agreeing a ten-year non-aggression period. The pact was broken when the Germans attacked the USSR in 1941.

Red Army: name of the Russian army set up by Trotsky during the Russian Civil War.

Korean War (1950–3): a conflict resulting from the partition of Korea into the Soviet-occupied North and the US-occupied South. It began when North Korean troops invaded the South.

> **How did he manage to become a significant contender for leadership by 1922?**

> **What part did economic policies play in his rise to power?**

> **How did personal and political rivalries affect his rise to power?**

Framework of events

1903	RSDLP split into Bolsheviks & Mensheviks
1912	Stalin elected to the Central Committee of the Bolshevik Party
	Stalin escaped from exile; edited party newspaper in St. Petersburg, before again being arrested and exiled
1917	Stalin became member of the Bolshevik Party Politburo
	Stalin appointed as People's Commissar for Nationalities
1918–21	Russian Civil War
1919	Stalin appointed as Head of the Workers' & Peasants' Inspectorate
1922	Stalin appointed as General Secretary of the Communist Party; in Triumvirate with Kamenev and Zinoviev
1924	Lenin's death
1925	Stalin's *Socialism In One Country* became official party policy
1926	Stalin's defeat of the Left: Trotsky, Zinoviev and Kamenev
1929–30	Stalin's defeat of the Right: Bukharin, Rykov and Tomsky

How Stalin managed to rise to power after Lenin's death has caused much contentious debate among historians. The structuralist school of historians emphasise the advantages that Stalin had within the bureaucratic state. Systems within the Communist Party, particularly Stalin's ability to accumulate power through the office of General Secretary, are seen as crucially important. Stalin's rise is viewed as the logical outcome of Communist Party organisation. Structuralist historian E. H. Carr suggests that it was 'a triumph, not of reason, but of organisation'.

Edward Hallet Carr, *A History of Soviet Russia* (Macmillan, 1978)

Written in 14 volumes covering the rise of the Bolshevik Party to 1929, E. H. Carr's hugely detailed work on Soviet Russia was a milestone in British studies of Bolshevik Russia and the USSR.

In the volume *Interregnum* E. H. Carr covered the transition in power from Lenin to Stalin in 1923–4. In *Socialism in One Country Volume 1, 1924–1926* he offered a detailed insight into the way that Stalin was able to defeat and isolate Trotsky.

These volumes remained the standard work on the rise of Stalin until the 1960s.

Fortunately E. H. Carr's huge work appeared in an abridged form entitled *The Russian Revolution from Lenin to Stalin, 1917–1929* produced by Carr's historian companion R. W. Davis in 1978.

The party history view agrees that Stalin gained power by dominating the party machine. However, greater emphasis is placed on Lenin as the originator of these administrative systems and their development, than on Stalin's effective manipulation of them in his rise to power. Since the collapse of the USSR, an increasingly comprehensive study of its archives has strengthened the party history view.

The liberal school of historians view the role of personality as paramount, believing that the actions of individuals, such as Lenin and Trotsky, and Stalin himself, were of more importance than party structures in Stalin's path to power. Stalin is seen as scheming, manipulative and ruthless, with all of his actions, including his ideological changes, defined by his pursuit of power. In contrast, his rivals are seen as having made foolish errors that enabled Stalin to triumph.

In 1992 the historian Norman Perreira summarised the debate in his article *Stalin and the Communist Party in the 1920s*. He questioned: 'Did the system spawn a monster – or a monster the system?'

How did Stalin manage to become a significant contender for leadership by 1922?

In post-revolutionary Russia Stalin was considered a moderate talent at best. In 1917 an exiled Menshevik described him as 'a grey blur'. Similarly, Trotsky believed that he was the Party's most 'eminent mediocrity'. Yet by 1922 Stalin had amassed a formidable range of posts and power, enough to be considered as a contender for leadership after Lenin's death.

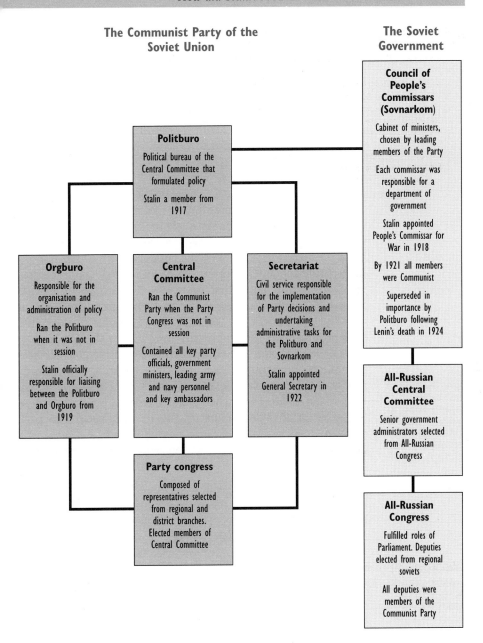

The Communist Party of the Soviet Union

The Soviet Government

Politburo

Political bureau of the Central Committee that formulated policy

Stalin a member from 1917

Orgburo

Responsible for the organisation and administration of policy

Ran the Politburo when it was not in session

Stalin officially responsible for liaising between the Politburo and Orgburo from 1919

Central Committee

Ran the Communist Party when the Party Congress was not in session

Contained all key party officials, government ministers, leading army and navy personnel and key ambassadors

Secretariat

Civil service responsible for the implementation of Party decisions and undertaking administrative tasks for the Politburo and Sovnarkom

Stalin appointed General Secretary in 1922

Party congress

Composed of representatives selected from regional and district branches. Elected members of Central Committee

Council of People's Commissars (Sovnarkom)

Cabinet of ministers, chosen by leading members of the Party

Each commissar was responsible for a department of government

Stalin appointed People's Commissar for War in 1918

By 1921 all members were Communist

Superseded in importance by Politburo following Lenin's death in 1924

All-Russian Central Committee

Senior government administrators selected from All-Russian Congress

All-Russian Congress

Fulfilled roles of Parliament. Deputies elected from regional soviets

All deputies were members of the Communist Party

The political structure of the Soviet Union in the mid-1920s.

The structuralist and party history interpretations emphasise the growth in the responsibilities dealt with by the Party as the machinery of the State enlarged. Chris Ward, in *Stalin's Russia* highlights how the Communist Party, which began as a mere 'debating society', became an organisation responsible for governing almost a sixth of the world. Administration and bureaucracy became more important than ideology. Stalin's increasingly influential position within these bureaucratic structures is viewed as the vital factor in his rise to power.

By 1917 Stalin was a member of the Politburo, the executive committee of the Bolshevik Party. In this position he drew up agendas, papers and minutes for the meetings through which he was able to influence discussions and the information that people received. By 1919 Stalin had become the official responsible for liaising between the Politburo and Orgburo. Within the Orgburo, Stalin could appoint supporters to key positions. Regional officials who met Stalin found that loyalty to him led to promotion, and further promotion depended on their loyalty. He was also appointed Head of the Workers' and Peasants' Inspectorate. This position allowed him a vast insight into the workings of central government departments. His appointment as People's Commissar for Nationalities in 1917 – a reward from Lenin for supporting his **April Theses** – made him a member of the Sovnarkom. From 1922, when Lenin appointed Stalin as General Secretary of the Communist Party, he dominated the party structure.

April Theses (1917): Lenin's ten-point programme outlining the continuation of the revolution against the Provisional Government.

Stalin in 1922

The structuralist view pinpoints Stalin's appointment as General Secretary of the Communist Party in April 1922 as the pivotal factor in his acquisition of power. This post allowed Stalin to influence events and people on a grand scale because, in the growing structure of state machinery, the centre of power became the Secretariat. Stalin was able to influence the selection of delegates to Party Congresses. This enabled him to 'pack' Congresses with his supporters and win votes for his policies. After 1924 Stalin led the '**Lenin Enrolment**', which almost doubled party membership and, by recruitment and expulsion, enabled him to exercise significant influence over the Communist Party. In *Stalin's Russia* (1993) Chris Ward argued that Trotsky 'might win the argument, but Stalin won the votes'. In exile, Trotsky wrote *The Revolution Betrayed* (1937) and argued that Marx's concept of a dictatorship of the **proletariat** had been twisted

Lenin Enrolment: a programme launched by Stalin to attract new members to the Communist Party to commemorate Lenin's death. The new recruits naturally supported the man who first admitted them to the party.

Proletariat: the urban working class.

into a dictatorship by the party bureaucracy, which from 1922 Stalin controlled. The historian, Robert Daniels, maintains that through a 'circular flow of power' Stalin created an essentially Stalinist Party at all levels of government.

Soon after Stalin's appointment as General Secretary, Lenin went into hospital and suffered several strokes. As Lenin grew increasingly ill, Stalin's importance rose dramatically.

What part did economic policies play in Stalin's rise to power?

From 1921 onwards, the Russian leadership was divided over economic policy. During the economic collapse and famine of 1921, Lenin abandoned the economic policy known as 'War Communism' and introduced his 'New Economic Policy' (NEP).

War Communism had been overtly communist. However, forced requisitioning of grain had led to mass peasant resistance. In contrast, under the NEP peasants were able to market surplus grain and, in Bukharin's words, 'enrich themselves'. During the reign of Tsar Nicolas II his Prime Minister, Peter Stolypin, encouraged the development of a richer **kulak** class among the peasants. Now it appeared that the communists were doing the same. Lenin's NEP was hugely controversial among the Communist Party. Many communists felt that they had not won power in the revolution, and held on to it in a bloody civil war, in order to revert to western-style capitalism and enable peasants to grow wealthy.

Kulaks: peasants who had been allowed to become wealthier either before the Revolutions of 1917 or during the NEP.

A temporary policy or the path to communism?

Historical debate arises as to which economic policy was the temporary measure that Lenin only resorted to because of circumstances. It

War Communism 1918–21	New Economic Policy 1921–28
Nationalisation of *all* industry	Large industries nationalised
Banning of private trade	Small firms privately owned for profit
Grain requisitioning in the countryside	Grain requisitioning abolished
Food rationing	Peasants gave some grain to the state as tax

Factory discipline
    e.g. fines
        use of internal passports
	Peasants allowed to market surplus grain and to become kulaks.

is disputed whether War Communism was a temporary policy for the duration of the Civil War, to be accepted whilst victory was ensured, or, as Evan Maudsley claims, 'the preferred policy of victorious Communism'. Similarly, the New Economic Policy can be regarded as nothing but a temporary u-turn, with its surprisingly capitalist features. Alternatively, it can be viewed as a policy put in place for some considerable time as Russia sought to find the correct path towards **socialism** and communism.

Socialism: an economic system in which the means of production, distribution and exchange are owned by the community collectively, usually through the state. A more moderate version of communism.

Nepmen: private traders or businessmen.

The economic debate: rightists v. leftists

When Lenin died, the collective leadership continued with his NEP. Unarguably, the NEP led to an economic revival. However, in the towns the new wealth was mainly in the hands of a new breed of entrepreneur, the **Nepmen**. Many party members were annoyed because the Nepmen were considered remnants of the old system. Trotsky, Kamenev and Zinoviev challenged the NEP and supported rapid industrial growth. Within the Party they led the leftist communists. Trotsky launched his attack on the NEP in October 1923. The west's intervention in the Russian Civil War had demonstrated that the USSR needed to industrialise, modernise and strengthen to be safe from hostile attack. Buying the machines for large scale industrialisation required selling as much grain abroad as possible. This could only be achieved by forcing the peasants to produce more grain for the state. Trotsky advocated driving peasants into collective farms to squeeze more

	The leftist communists	The rightist communists
Attitude to NEP	■ A temporary policy due to be scrapped	■ A permanent policy whilst the USSR recovered stability
Main arguments	■ Need to industrialise rapidly	■ Need a time of recovery after the upheaval of war and civil war
	■ Need to squeeze grain from peasants to obtain foreign capital to pay for industrialisation	■ Build towards socialism gradually at a pace that works
	■ Need to encourage revolution abroad in order to end the USSR's international isolation	■ Allow the Kulaks and Nepmen to grow richer – let the profit incentive aid Soviet economic recovery
Main advocates	■ Trotsky ■ Zinoviev ■ Kamenev	■ Bukharin ■ Rykov ■ Tomsky

grain out of them, and establishing compulsory labour units to kick-start rapid industrialisation. As well as revolutionising the Russian economy and society, Trotsky wanted 'Permanent Revolution', to export communism abroad.

Trotsky's argument, the leftist view, made sense. However, the rightists, led by Bukharin, Rykov and Tomsky, believed that after the chaos and dislocation of war, revolution and civil war, the USSR needed a time of stability and recovery. Bukharin thought that it would be decades before the USSR would be ready for the sort of policies that Trotsky was advocating. He stated: 'we shall ride to socialism at the speed of the peasant horse'. War Communism had led to widespread peasant resistance and then to the famine of 1921. This gave the rightist arguments a great deal of popular appeal.

In December 1924 Stalin advocated the policy of 'Socialism In One Country', a direct contradiction to Trotsky's Permanent Revolution. Stalin argued that world revolution was not on the agenda. Recent world events seemed to confirm that he was right: the crushing of the only other temporarily successful communist revolution in Hungary; the defeat of the German **Spartacists** in 1919; the rise of **Mussolini** and fascism in Italy. Stalin argued that the USSR should concentrate on developing socialism (note: not communism) on her own. Stalin appealed to the patriotic pride of the people, asserting that the USSR would show the world what socialism meant. He implied that Trotsky had a very poor opinion of the capability of the Soviet people if he believed that they had to wait for revolutions to be successful in other countries before establishing socialism in the USSR. In *Bukharin and the Bolshevik Revolution* (1971), Stephen Cohen argued that 'machine politics alone did not account for Stalin's triumph' and stressed that Stalin's cultivation of 'Bolshevism's heroic tradition' won him support. At the Fourteenth Party Congress in April 1925 it was Stalin's policy of Socialism In One Country, rather than Trotsky's Permanent Revolution, that became official policy.

Historians of the liberal school claim that Stalin's continuation of the NEP, through his advocacy of Socialism In One Country, demonstrates his political abilities. Stalin kept the NEP while it served its industrial purpose. Liberal historians argue that Stalin took the right stance in attacking Trotsky's hardline proposals. The prospect of further struggle and permanent revolution was highly unattractive to many contemporaries. By bridging the gap between the radical extremes, Stalin demonstrated his practical political skill. Once his catchy phrase became party policy, any future

Spartacist: a movement founded in 1916 and reorganised as the German Communist Party in November 1918 with the aim of overthrowing capitalism by a revolutionary rising of German workers. All attempts were suppressed.

Mussolini (1883–1945) Italian dictator who founded fascism in 1919. Fascism encouraged militarism and nationalism, organising the country along authoritaran lines.

Factionalism: in the context of the USSR a faction is a sub-group that campaigns against official party policy. In 1921 the organising of sub-groups or factionalism was banned by Lenin.

opposition to it could be quashed as forbidden **factionalism**, which Lenin had banned in 1921 at the Tenth Party Congress.

By 1928, Stalin was abandoning Socialism in One Country and the NEP and implementing the policies of the expelled leftists. When the rightists such as Bukharin objected, they too were expelled for factionalism. Liberal historians like Robert Conquest and Robert Tucker argue that Stalin manipulated the ideological disputes to his best advantage. His adoption of Socialism In One Country and the Five-Year Plans were simply devices to win power. Party historians stress that it was Lenin's banning of factions in 1921 that enabled Stalin to expel his rivals.

How did personal and political rivalries affect Stalin's rise to power?

The liberal view suggests that the personalities of Stalin's key rivals, and the mistakes that they made, facilitated his rise to power. Stalin's manipulation of people, situations and ideology is also stressed. They also question Lenin's role, particularly his failure to remove Stalin from his position as General Secretary despite his misgivings about him.

Why did Lenin's growing opposition to Stalin not prevent his rise to power?

From 1922 Stalin's power base was threatened by Lenin's realisation that he had given Stalin too much power and that his own system was creating a monster. The roots of Lenin's distrust can perhaps be found in some of Stalin's previous mistakes. After February 1917, as Editor of *Pravda*, Stalin supported Russia's involvement in the First World War – a view not shared by Lenin. During the Russian Civil War, Stalin was also removed from organising the defence of Tsaritsyn (later Stalingrad) for disobeying Trotsky's orders. Lastly, it emerged that Stalin had a different agenda to Lenin with regards to the future of the Russian Empire. Bolshevik propaganda before 1917 suggested that the minority nations of the Russian Empire might gain the right to independent self-government. In January 1918, a new constitution renamed the country the Russian Soviet Federal Socialist Republic (RSFSR). This existed only in the heart of Russia until 1920, because throughout the Civil War most of the outer areas of the RSFSR were in the hands of the Whites. As they were recaptured, areas like the Ukraine and Georgia became separate **republics**. Lenin planned that these republics would be

Republic: a country without a monarchy.

Federal system:
A system of government where states are united and have a central government but considerable power and authority is given to the individual states.

united in a **federal system**. This occurred in 1922 when the Union of the Soviet Socialist Republics (USSR) was established. As Commissar for Nationalities since 1917, Stalin had different plans. Despite his own Georgian origins, he wanted these republics to be directly controlled from Moscow. Stalin turned his back on his native roots, referred to Georgia as 'a little piece of Soviet territory' and imposed brutal 'russification', which appalled Lenin.

Lenin's Political Testament

After his second stroke in December 1922, Lenin dictated 'A Letter to Congress', which became known as his 'Political Testament'. It was his review of the current position of the USSR with some indication of future plans. The testament was particularly damning about Stalin:

> 'Comrade Stalin, having become Secretary General, has unlimited authority concentrated in his hand, and I am not sure he will always be capable of using that power with sufficient caution.'

25 December 1922

> 'Stalin is too rude and this defect becomes intolerable in a General Secretary. I suggest that the comrades think about a way of removing Stalin and appointing another man in his stead who in all other respects differs from Comrade Stalin.'

Postscript 4 January 1923

This testament could instantaneously have destroyed Stalin's credibility if made public. However, as Lenin's health collapsed, it remained in a sealed envelope in the care of his wife, Krupskaya.

What Lenin apparently did not know when he wrote these damning comments was that Stalin had deeply offended Krupskaya on 22 December 1922. Stalin had discovered that Lenin had written to Trotsky to congratulate him on a victory in a policy debate. This enraged Stalin, who rang Krupskaya and was very abusive. Lenin did not learn about Stalin's behaviour until March 1923. Lenin immediately wrote to Stalin – copying the letter for Zinoviev and Kamenev:

> 'Very respectable Comrade Stalin, you allowed yourself to be so ill-mannered … It goes without saying what was done against my wife I also consider to have been directed against myself.'

Lenin's objections to Stalin had now deepened on a personal level. Although Stalin made a sort of an apology, he effectively denied all

Krupskaya's claims about his rudeness. Both Trotsky and Kamenev were then leaked information from Lenin's secretaries that Lenin was preparing 'a bomb' for Stalin which would politically crush him.

When the Twelfth Congress of the Communist Party met in April 1923, Lenin's Political Testament lay purposefully sealed in its envelope. Before the next Congress met, Lenin had died.

Stalin's political rivals

Treaty of Brest-Litovsk (1918): peace agreement negotiated with Germany. Russia lost nearly 20 per cent of its territory and roughly 25 per cent of its population.

When Lenin died on 21 January 1924 Leon Trotsky was his 'heir apparent': his right-hand man, the architect of the October Revolution and tireless organiser of victory in the Russian Civil War. Yet there were other key and influential figures rivalling Trotsky and Stalin for accession to leadership.

Stalin's Rivals

Nikolai Bukharin (1888–1938)
- Joined Bolsheviks in 1906
- Arrested in 1912; escaped and remained abroad until 1917
- Opposed Lenin over the **Treaty of Brest-Litovsk**
- Leading supporter of the New Economic Policy (NEP), introduced in 1921
- In Lenin's favour; Lenin called him the 'golden boy of the Bolshevik Party'
- Arrested and executed in 1938

Lev Kamenev (1883–1936)
- Joined Bolsheviks in 1905
- In exile with Lenin from 1907 to 1914; exiled in Siberia from 1914 to 1917
- Disagreed with Lenin in 1917; opposed Lenin's 'April Theses' and plans for the armed uprising in October
- Head of Moscow Soviet; Commissar for Foreign Trade
- Opposed the NEP
- Member of anti-Trotsky Triumvirate in 1922
- Accused of Kirov's murder in 1936 and executed

Gregory Zinoviev (1883–1936)
- Joined Bolsheviks after 1903 split
- In exile with Lenin until April 1917
- Openly opposed the October rising
- Resigned from Bolshevik government because Lenin refused to form a coalition including left-socialist parties

- Party Secretary in Petrograd; Chairman of Comintern (set up to spread communism internationally in 1919); Member of Politburo in 1921
- Leading opponent of the NEP
- Member of Triumvirate in 1922
- Accused of Kirov's murder and executed in 1936

Alexei Rykov (1881–1938)

- Secretly supported plans for coalition government in 1917
- People's Commissar for the Interior 1917–18; member of Politburo in 1924; Chairman of the Supreme Council for the National Economy from 1918–20 and 1923–4
- Elected to succeed Lenin as Chairman of Sovnarkom and Prime Minister of the USSR
- Leading supporter of the NEP
- Arrested and executed in 1938

Leon Trotsky (1879–1940)

- Arrested and exiled to Siberia in 1900; escaped and joined the Social Democratic Party
- Did not back Lenin during the 1903 Party split
- Leading role in the 1905 Revolution; Chairman of the Petrograd Soviet
- Spent the years to 1917 abroad; in USA at the time of the **February Revolution**;
- Returned to Russia in 1917 and joined the Bolsheviks; swiftly became Lenin's right-hand man
- The main architect of the October Revolution
- Chaired the Military Revolutionary Committee of the Petrograd Soviet and significantly changed Lenin's revolutionary plans
- As Commissar for Foreign Affairs negotiated the Treaty of Brest-Litovsk with Germany in March 1918
- From March 1918 acted as Commissar for War; created the Red Army; led the Communists to victory against the Whites by 1920
- Elected to the Politburo in 1919
- Supporter of 'International Revolution'
- Major opponent of the NEP
- Ousted from the Communist Party and expelled from Russia in 1929; assassinated in 1940

February Revolution: this involved the abdication of Tsar Nicholas II and the end of the Romanov dynasty. The Tsar was replaced by a Provisional Government.

Although Trotsky stood out as Stalin's main rival for power after Lenin's death, he made a catalogue of mistakes which liberal historians believe contributed greatly to Stalin's rise to power.

After the split in the RSDLP in 1903, Trotsky waited until 1917 to join the Bolshevik Party. This caused other Bolsheviks to mistrust his devotion to the cause. By 1922 Trotsky's contribution to the Communist Party's consolidation of power in the USSR was second-to-none, yet he refused Lenin's offer of making him deputy, a post which would certainly have strengthened his position. This typifies the mistakes that Trotsky repetively made. In October 1923 Trotsky attacked the Triumvirate. He had two main criticisms. First, he opposed the New Economic Policy (NEP) as a partial return to capitalism and the abandonment of communist principles. Liberal historians suggest that this outspoken critique of Lenin's policy caused others to distrust him. Secondly, Trotsky felt that appointments from above were replacing elections from below which led to an 'unhealthy regime'. Forty-six other communists signed Trotsky's statement, which led to accusations of factionalism. Trotsky's attack on the Triumvirate meant that an alliance between the three key leftists (Kamenev, Zinoviev and Trotsky) in the Communist Party was even more unlikely at this critical juncture. This undoubtedly helped Stalin in his quest for power.

In the winter of 1923–4 Trotsky was ill with a malarial infection. On 18 January 1924, he caught a train south to recuperate. Three days later, Lenin died. Trotsky's train was at the station in Georgia, when he received a coded message from Stalin telling him that Lenin was dead. Isaac Deutscher has described the fatal miscalculation that Trotsky made that day in *The Prophet Unarmed: Trotsky 1921–29*. He outlines how Stalin lied about the date of the funeral, claiming that Trotsky would never make it on time. His absence at the ceremony is viewed as a tactical failure. Only the Triumvirate featured and Trotsky, it was felt, could not be bothered to turn up. Deutscher claimed: 'It was a political error of the first magnitude and dealt a fatal blow to Trotsky's prestige'.

The impact of Lenin's death

Deification: to personify someone as God.

To make matters worse for Trotsky, Lenin's death was followed by his near-**deification** in the USSR. Stalin gave the funeral oration and spoke of Lenin as though he was God:

'Comrade Lenin ordered us to maintain and strengthen the dictatorship of the proletariat … In leaving us, Comrade Lenin ordered us to strengthen with all our might the union of workers

A real friendship — or a
doctored photograph?

and peasants. We swear to thee, Comrade Lenin, to honour thy command.'

As the cult of Lenin gained momentum, the decision was taken to preserve his body and display it in a mausoleum in Red Square. Stalin launched the Lenin Enrolment to increase party membership, and the leading lights of the party fell over each other in attempting to praise Lenin loudest and longest. Interestingly, each seemed to feel that their policies were the preferred policies of their glorious leader. Stalin simply did this best, setting himself up as Lenin's disciple. He certainly convinced the majority of the Soviet people.

The Thirteenth Party Congress

Lenin's damnation of Stalin remained recorded in his Political Testament. If Lenin's views had become public while he was still alive, Stalin would have been finished.

In May 1924, just before the Thirteenth Party Congress, Krupskaya sent the testament to Kamenev. She informed Kamenev that Lenin had wished his 'personal appraisals' of 'some Central Committee members' to be presented at the Congress. The leadership decided that the testament was to be read aloud by Kamenev to the Central Committee, just before the Party Congress. However, none of the Party members were entirely happy with the content. Michael Lynch in *Stalin and Khrushchev: The USSR 1924–64* (1990) argues that 'nearly all of the members of the Politburo had reasons for suppressing the testament'. Lenin had not only attacked Stalin. Trotsky heard about his 'excess of self-confidence'. Kamenev and Zinoviev must have choked at Lenin describing Trotsky and Stalin as 'these two outstanding leaders', despite his other criticisms of them. Lenin also described Bukharin as 'the most valuable and most able theorist' who should be 'the favourite of the whole party'. Virtually all of the others were embarassed by how Lenin had described them. Zinoviev described every word of Lenin as sacred, but went on to clear Stalin's name. Kamenev echoed his support for Stalin. Trotsky remained silent. Stalin offered to resign from the post of General Secretary. His resignation was rejected unanimously. The Central Committee decided that Lenin had been very ill when he wrote the testament and that it should neither be read in Congress nor published. Undoubtedly they were shielding their embarassment. Kamenev and Zinoviev made the crucial error of retaining Stalin, believing that this would help them to prevent Trotsky's emergence as dictator.

Stalin's survival and Trotsky's decline

Of all of the leaders, Trotsky lost the most. In *The Prophet Unarmed: Trotsky 1921–29* (1959) Isaac Deutscher suggested that perhaps Trotsky fatally underestimated Stalin: 'It seemed almost a bad joke to Trotsky that Stalin, the shabby and inarticulate man in the background, should be his rival'.

Trotsky's future swiftly declined. At the Thirteenth Partty Congress he renewed his attacks on party policy but was roundly defeated by a Congress packed with Stalinist delegates. In 1924, during the so-called 'Literary Wars', Stalin published *On The Foundations of Leninism* in which he claimed that Stalinism was Leninism and condemned Trotsky for disloyalty to Lenin. Various literary attacks between Trotsky, Zinoviev and Kamenev ensued. Stalin attacked Trotsky's theory of Permanent Revolution as treacherous. By the end of 1924, Trotsky was publicly under attack and regularly denounced at Party meetings. In January 1925 he was replaced as Commissar for War.

The 'united opposition' and its decline

At the Fourteenth Party Congress in April 1925 Stalin's policy of Socialism In One Country became party policy. Kamenev and Zinoviev were now also in trouble. Despite being leading members of the Triumvirate, the adoption of Socialism In One Country directly contradicted their own leftist views. It did not take long for their predicament to become apparent. During 1925 they both publicly stated that it would need victorious revolutions in the leading capitalist nations before the USSR could achieve socialism. By the end of 1925, a year of bumper harvests, Zinoviev was calling for an end to the NEP and rapid industrialisation.

These protests propelled Stalin's launch of successful attacks on the left in 1926. Too late, Trotsky, Zinoviev and Kamenev chose to forget their personal differences to form the 'United Opposition'. Following defeats at the Party Congress, Zinoviev and Kamenev lost their posts as Party Secretaries in Leningrad and Moscow, replaced by Stalin's supporters, Kirov and Molotov.

By December 1926 Stalin was the only member of the Triumvirate still in the Politburo. By 1927 Trotsky was expelled from the Communist Party and exiled to Kazakhstan, before being exiled abroad in 1929. Thus Stalin's main rival had been defeated. It is arguable that Stalin had already won power. The Politburo now consisted of new boys who owed their advancement to Stalin, and

old guard rightists who had backed Stalin's policy of Socialism In One Country in 1925, and his attacks on the left in 1926.

In 1928 Stalin made his move against the rightists. He suddenly switched his economic stance and adopted the policies of the leftists by launching the Five-Year Plans and collectivisation. When Bukharin, Rykov and Tomsky objected, they were condemned and dismissed for factionalism. In September 1928 Bukharin launched an attack on the new policies in *Notes of an Economist*. In 1929 he lost the Chairmanship of Comintern, the editorship of *Pravda* and was dismissed from the Politburo. Tomsky and Rykov were removed from their posts and, in 1930, lost their seats in the Politburo.

A cartoon mocking the 'united opposition'.

Stalin in power

In Stalin's lifetime Soviet historians argued that Stalin had personally saved the USSR from scheming 'enemies of the people' such as Trotsky. This however is **hagiography** not **historiography.** In 1919 the American journalist John Reed, who was in Russia during the October Revolution, described Stalin as 'not an intellectual, but he knows what he wants. He's got willpower and he's going to be top of the pile some day'. In his article *Stalin and the Communist Party in the 1920s* (1992), Norman Perreira concluded that the 1920s 'ended with Stalin alone at the helm. Still no one imagined the full terrible consequences of what was to follow … [and celebrated] the occasion of Stalin's fiftieth birthday on December 21st 1929, just as his revolution from above was descending upon their heads'. Had the system spawned a monster – or a monster the system? In *Stalin's Russia* (1999) Chris Ward argues that the various views of Stalin's rise to power should not be seen as 'mutually exclusive interpretations' and that 'no single factor can satisfactorily explain Stalin's rise'.

Hagiography: a completely uncritical view of the subject being studied.

Historiography: the actual history of the study of history. Understanding the way in which interpretations of a topic have changed through time.

How did Stalin become leader of the USSR?

1. Read the following extract and answer the question.

   'In 1924 Trotsky launched an attack on the growth of the party bureaucracy. He highlighted the danger of the bureaucracy becoming a class in itself, which would work for its own benefit. Trotsky's criticisms of the bureaucracy were unpopular in the party and consequently Stalin was able to isolate him. One factor in his favour was Lenin's rule against factionalism. Stalin could always use the accusation of factionalism to frustrate opposition within the party. It was a weapon he was to use to good effect against his opponents when differences arose over ideology and policy.'

   (adapted from Steven Phillips *Stalinist Russia*, Heinemann, 2000)

   Using information in the extract above, and from this chapter, explain how Communist Party rules and structures helped Stalin rise to power.

2. Why was Stalin rather than Trotsky able to gain power in Russia after Lenin's death?

Stalin's foreign policy: defensive or expansionist?

1924–41: Was his main aim Soviet security?

Was he primarily responsible for the Cold War?

How did the Second World War affect his foreign policy?

Was his foreign policy successful?

Framework of events

1922	Treaty of Rapallo
1924	The 'Zinoviev Letter' published
1926	Treaty of Berlin
1933	Hitler became Chancellor of Germany
1934	USSR joined the League of Nations
1935	Mutual assistance treaties with France and Czechoslovakia
1939	Nazi – Soviet Pact
1941	Barbarossa – German invasion of the USSR
1941–5	The Great Patriotic War (Second World War)
1941–4	Siege of Leningrad
1942–3	Battle of Stalingrad
1943	Teheran Conference
1945	Yalta and Potsdam Conferences
1946	Iron Curtain speech
1947	Truman Doctrine and Marshall Aid
1948	Czechoslovakian Coup
1948–9	Berlin Blockade and Airlift
1949	USSR tested its first atomic bomb
1950–3	The Korean War

1924–41: Was Stalin's main aim Soviet security?

Two aims in foreign policy emerged after the Russian Revolutions: to spread world communism and to defend the USSR from its enemies. Between 1922 and 1941 the USSR was vulnerable, being the only communist state in an essentially hostile capitalist world. In his 1931 *Pravda* article Stalin wrote: 'We are ... years behind the advanced countries. We must make good this distance in ten years. Either we do it, or they crush us.' Although Trotsky had advocated permanent revolution during the 1920s, Stalin's priorities were increasingly modernisation, security and defence.

The Comintern

Comintern: The Communist International set up in 1919 to coordinate the activities of communist parties worldwide.

In 1919 Lenin's **Comintern** had been set up to spread communism internationally. Most historians argue that after the introduction of Stalin's policy of Socialism In One Country in 1925, the USSR turned its back on world revolution. In 1990 Michael Lynch argued that the USSR had never been in a position to seriously advance the cause of international communism, and that this did not become a realistic goal again until towards the end of the Second World War. In *The Comintern: A History of International Communism from Lenin to Stalin* (1996), McDermott and Agnew outline 'Stalin's notorious disdain for foreign communists, for the Comintern as a whole'. Chris Ward, in *Stalin's Russia, 2nd edition* (1999), argued that 'Stalin never believed in international revolution and viewed the Comintern merely as a means of advancing Moscow's foreign policy schemes'. The Comintern became a tool for keeping foreign communist parties in line with Stalin's own policies.

From 1918 Germany and Russia were Europe's outcasts. Georgi Chicherin, the anti-British Commissar for Foreign Affairs (1918–30), believed that Germany was the USSR's natural ally. Lenin had negotiated the Treaty of Rapallo with Germany in 1922. Stalin further strengthened these links through trade agreements and the **Treaty of Berlin** (1926). Relations with Britain were problematical. The USSR gained diplomatic recognition in 1924. However, later that year *The Times* newspaper published a forged letter, supposedly written by Zinoviev, calling for British communists to wage 'class war', which strained Russo-British relations. Diplomatic recognition was cut in 1927 and not restored until the formation of Britain's second Labour Government in 1929.

Treaty of Berlin (1926): agreement between Germany and the Soviet Union in which both pledged neutrality in the event of an attack on the other by a third party.

The conventional wisdom in the USSR was that the worsening depression in Germany after 1929 would lead to the triumph of communism. This was true to an extent because the early 1930s saw support for the Communist Party (KPD) rise at the polls. The KPD finished second in the election of July 1932, but the Comintern imposed a policy of non-cooperation with the Social Democrats, who were to be attacked as 'social fascists'. This ended

**Adolf Hitler
(1889–1945)**
The Austrian-born dictator of Germany. Became leader of the Nazi party in 1920 and German Chancellor in 1933. Hitler created the extreme right-wing political ideology of **Nazism**, which included the principles of Aryan superiority, the Germans being considered as the 'master race'; a policy of anti-communism; anti-Semitism and racism; the building up of the armed forces; and a determination to regain lost territory.

The League of Nations (1919): an international organisation set up to preserve the peace and settle disputes by discussion and agreement.

Rome-Berlin Axis (1936): the informal alliance between Italy and Germany.

Anti-Comintern Pact: an anti-Communist alliance.

any hope of preventing the anti-communist **Hitler** from being appointed as German Chancellor in 1933. His scrapping of Rapallo and the trade agreements was economically damaging considering that 47 per cent of the USSR's imports came from Germany in 1932. However, the potential political consequences were much worse. Faced with the threat of **Nazism**, The USSR was diplomatically isolated.

The search for 'collective security', 1933–9

The rise of Nazism forced the USSR to revise its foreign policy. The extent to which Stalin was personally responsible for those changes is the subject of historical debate. In 1938 historian Franz Borkenau argued that Stalin maintained personal control over the Comintern and foreign policy. Other historians, such as E. H. Carr in *Twilight of the Comintern* (1982), have described Stalin as an 'absentee director' who rarely intervened because his main focus was on domestic affairs. D. C. Watt argues that until the Munich Conference of 1938 Stalin allowed Maxim Litvinov, Commissar for Foreign Affairs (1930–1939), to control foreign policy.

A Jew and anti-German, Litvinov favoured a policy of collective security with the west against the threat of Nazism. In 1934 Stalin and Litvinov took the USSR into the **League of Nations**. In 1935, with the aim of containing Germany, the USSR signed treaties with France and Czechoslovakia, promising mutual assistance against attack. From August 1935 the Communist Parties in the capitalist states were ordered to set up 'popular front' coalitions with socialists. However, regaining the trust of those previously branded as 'social fascists' proved difficult. By 1936 the League of Nations was discredited. The **Rome-Berlin Axis** of 1936, and the subsequent alignment of Germany, Italy and Japan in the **Anti-Comintern Pact**, placed the USSR in a vulnerable position. An alternative to collective security was urgently required. The USSR needed allies.

The search for allies

A number of western historians in the Germanist school, such as R. Tucker, have argued that Stalin's aim from 1933 was to revitalise the German alliance. Historians in the collective security school believe that the USSR genuinely sought collective security against Nazism from 1933. Historian Geoffrey Roberts argued that despite wanting alliances with Britain and France, Stalin was deeply suspicious of their motives.

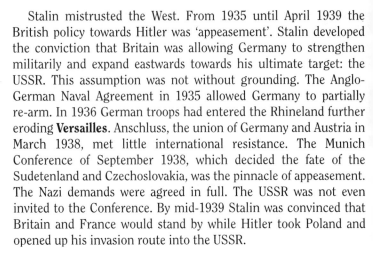

Stalin mistrusted the West. From 1935 until April 1939 the British policy towards Hitler was 'appeasement'. Stalin developed the conviction that Britain was allowing Germany to strengthen militarily and expand eastwards towards his ultimate target: the USSR. This assumption was not without grounding. The Anglo-German Naval Agreement in 1935 allowed Germany to partially re-arm. In 1936 German troops had entered the Rhineland further eroding **Versailles**. Anschluss, the union of Germany and Austria in March 1938, met little international resistance. The Munich Conference of September 1938, which decided the fate of the Sudetenland and Czechoslovakia, was the pinnacle of appeasement. The Nazi demands were agreed in full. The USSR was not even invited to the Conference. By mid-1939 Stalin was convinced that Britain and France would stand by while Hitler took Poland and opened up his invasion route into the USSR.

> **Versailles (1919):** a treaty which imposed war-guilt and punishment on Germany. By the 1930s the terms were widely regarded as too harsh. This enabled Hitler to present his demands as 'reasonable'.

The Nazi-Soviet Pact (August 1939)

Neville Chamberlain also mistrusted Stalin. After Hitler broke the Munich Agreement in March 1939, by dismantling the remainder of Czechoslovakia, Chamberlain dispatched a military mission for talks in Moscow despite his distrust of Stalin. In stark contrast to Chamberlain's own personal diplomacy with Hitler, who he flew to Germany to see three times in September 1938, the mission to Moscow consisted of second-raters who travelled by boat and train. This confirmed Stalin's worst fears concerning Britain's intentions, and provoked his signing of the Nazi-Soviet Pact, a ten-year non-aggression agreement.

> **Neville Chamberlain (1869–1940)** A Conservative politician and British PM from 1937 to 1940. He followed a policy of 'appeasement' towards Nazi Germany, and signed the Munich Agreement. The policy was unsuccessful in curbing Hitler's aggressive policies, which led to the Second World War. Dissatisfaction with Chamberlain's wartime leadership led to his resignation in 1940.

In *Stalin and Khrushchev: The USSR, 1924–64* (1990) Michael Lynch described how 'the impossible had occurred; the sworn ideological enemies, Nazi Germany and Communist Russia, had come together'. The Pact made sense to both countries at the time, and in restoring a 'friendly' relationship between the USSR and Germany it was consistent with Soviet policy between 1922 and 1933. In April 1939 Viacheslav Molotov replaced Litvinov as Commissar for Foreign Affairs. He advocated improved relations with Germany. The Germanists have sought to demonstrate a consistency of aim in foreign policy, but the view of the collective security school is that Stalin pragmatically chose the alliance that offered the most security to the USSR.

Both sides benefited from the agreement. It 'appeared' to safeguard the USSR from attack and enabled Germany to fight in the west without fearing attack by the USSR. The treaty also

A contemporary British view of the Nazi-Soviet Pact entitled 'Rendevous'. Poland lies helpless between Hitler and Stalin.

contained secret territorial clauses, including the carve-up of Poland and permission for the USSR to regain the Baltic territories lost at Brest-Litovsk. Alan Bullock believes that 'the decisive element which led Stalin to prefer the German proposal was something that the British and French could never have matched – a share not in the defence of an ungrateful Eastern Europe's independence, but in its partition, and this in return for the USSR standing aside, for agreeing not to enter any war which might break out' (see **Landmark Study** p 34).

However, the USSR also lost a great deal, most significantly the existence of Poland as a buffer state between them and their worst nightmare – Nazism. For a time, as the Nazis conquered much of western Europe and came close to defeating Britain, the USSR seemed to be emerging unscathed. However, this changed in 1941 when Germany invaded the USSR on 22 June.

If expanding communism was the goal in this period then Stalin's foreign policy cannot be viewed as successful. However, if protecting the USSR was the key aim then he was probably as successful as possible given the circumstances, especially considering Britain's reluctance to seriously consider an alliance.

Alan Bullock, *Hitler And Stalin: Parallel Lives* (HarperCollins Publishers, 1998)

Bullock's book deals with all facets of Stalin's life from childhood to death. He makes sharp observations when comparing the two dictators. His chapters on 'Lenin's Successor' and 'Stalin's Revolution' contain thorough observations and excellent insights into Stalin's rise to power and his domestic policies in the 1930s. Bullock stresses the pragmatic nature of Stalin's policies towards Hitler. He also sees Stalin as willing to take action over the Sudetenland as long as it was in co-operation with the west. After Munich, Bullock argues that collective security had clearly failed and that by the time the British attempted to re-build collective security after the taking of Czechoslovakia in the spring of 1939, Stalin was 'convinced that Britain and France were seeking to encourage conflict between Germany and Russia'. Bullock views Stalin as weighing up his choices in the summer of 1939 between a pact with Britain and France and dealing with Hitler. Bullock sees Stalin as taking the best deal on offer for the USSR in 1939.

For Stalin, the Nazi-Soviet Pact was probably his only option in August 1939. Nevertheless, the wisdom of Stalin trusting the anti-communist Hitler is questionable.

How did the Second World War affect Stalin's foreign policy?

Operation Barbarossa: The Nazi codename for the invasion of the USSR.

The Great War (1914–18): in which Russia fought alongside Britain and France until surrendering to Germany in the Treaty of Brest-Litovsk.

From the moment that Hitler launched **Operation Barbarossa** it was portrayed within the USSR as the **Great Patriotic War**. In *Stalin's Russia, 2nd Edition* (1999) Chris Ward has highlighted two interpretative viewpoints, 'negative' and 'positive', in relation to research into how the Great Patriotic War impacted on the USSR and how the USSR was able to emerge victorious. The negative view emphasises the incompetence and disorganisation of the USSR, especially in 1941, and the errors and failures of the Germans. The positive view emphasises the effectiveness of the USSR's response to Barbarossa and the extraordinary resilience that characterised the Soviet war effort.

The negative view highlights Stalin's inept leadership in June 1941. Seemingly caught off-guard, Stalin retired to his dacha. By the time Stalin returned to the helm, a million Soviet soldiers had died. Stalin further weakened the command structure of the Red Army by executing front-line generals. Chris Ward comments that Stalin 'continually obstructed the High Command and interfered in matters beyond his competence'.

History and the weather saved Stalin. Twice previously the Russian Empire had defeated invasions. On both occasions the Russians defended their country by burning all crops that the invader might live off, an action known as 'scorched earth tactics'. The USSR's size and the severity of the winter also caused real damage to the invaders. In the summer of 1941 a more modern variant of 'scorched earth' tactics was employed, including the dismantling and removal of 1500 factories beyond the Ural Mountains. The German advance drew them into the depth of the USSR as winter approached. By September, Leningrad was under siege. By October, the attack on Moscow was underway. Without winter uniforms, and with their tanks unusable because the diesel froze, the German attack came to a standstill in the winter of 1941–2 and Moscow was saved.

Although Hitler miscalculated when he invaded the USSR, his defeat was not inevitable, especially during 1942. In this year, Germany switched their main attack southwards towards **Stalingrad** where it ground to a halt. The counter-attacking Soviets trapped the German Sixth Army in Stalingrad. Hitler ordered them to stand and fight when westwards retreat was the only hope. Stalin ordered his men to defend Stalingrad. At **Kursk**, the biggest tank battle of the Second World War, the Soviets won another pivotal victory. In Churchill's words: 'The Russians tore the guts out of the German army'. In 1944–5 the Soviets systematically drove the Germans back, first from the USSR and then through Eastern Europe. By early 1945, Soviet troops launched the final assault on Berlin.

The negative view emphasises the severity of the Soviet winters and German tactical and strategic errors such as at Stalingrad. Nazi racism contributed to the German defeat. The Ukrainians initially welcomed the German Army as 'liberators' but the German treatment of all Slavs as sub-human, and their use of millions of conquered Soviets as slave-labour, soon ensured a hatred of all things German.

The positive view emphasises Stalin's leadership and the resilience of the USSR during the war. In *Stalin* (1966) Isaac Deutscher praises Stalin: 'He solidly armed his country and re-organised its military forces. He had achieved absolute unity of command, the dream of the modern strategist'. In *The Soviet Home Front 1941–45* (1991) John Barber and Mark Harrison stressed the organisational achievements in industry and agriculture during the war. The development of the economy in the 1930s enabled the USSR to swiftly recover from the devastating impact of Operation Barbarossa. From 1941 to 1945 ten million people were evacuated to the huge new industrial centres situated east of the Urals. Munitions output doubled in 1942 and peaked in 1944. By 1943 the USSR produced more war material than Germany. Aid received from the USSR's wartime allies also contributed to the victory.

Equally impressive was the heroism, morale and patriotism of the

Stalingrad: the scene of a huge Soviet victory after the Germans besieged the city (1942–3). The battle marked the decisive end of German territorial advance on the Eastern Front.

Kursk (1943): A huge tank battle in which Soviet forces defeated the last major German offensive on Soviet soil.

Soviet people in the face of enormous suffering. Undoubtedly propaganda steeled the Soviet people for sacrifice, as did the relaxation of collectivisation and the restrictions on religion in pursuit of national unity. In *I Chose Freedom* (1947) Vic Kravchenko described how the USSR was gripped by a 'mighty surge of patriotism that came from the profoundest depths of Russian history and the Russian soul'. Yet he concluded: 'It had nothing to do with Stalin'.

Was Stalin primarily responsible for the Cold War?

The wartime Grand Alliance between the USSR, the USA and Britain, faced the axis powers of Germany, Italy and Japan. However, the Grand Alliance was forged by circumstance rather than choice. The USSR was dragged into the war by Operation Barbarossa. **Pearl Harbor** brought the USA into the conflict. The leaders of the Grand Alliance – Stalin, **Roosevelt** and **Churchill** – were united by one common goal – victory. Beyond that there were inevitable tensions arising from their huge differences, in terms of ideology and their actual wartime experience. Political differences – between capitalist democracy and communist dictatorship – underpinned these disputes which, by 1945, were spiralling into the suspicion and hostility that formed the basis of the Cold War.

Pearl Harbor (1941): the main US naval base which was attacked by the Japanese provoking the US declaration of war. Within days Japan's allies, Germany and Italy declared war on the USA.

Why and how the wartime alliance collapsed so dramatically into Cold War enmity has been the subject of intense debate between historians since the 1940s. In 1987 in *Perestroika: New Thinking for Our Country and the World* (1987) Gorbachev, the leader of the USSR, wrote: 'when one country sees another as evil incarnate, and itself as the embodiment of absolute good, relations between them have reached a stalemate'. Both the USA, supported by Britain, and the USSR held this view. Despite their wartime alliance, conflict was almost inevitable.

the US Democratic president from 1933 to 1945. He was elected president four times, a unique achievement He has been criticised for his readiness to give in to Stalin.

Franklin Delano Roosevelt (1882–1945)

British Prime Minister from 1940 to 1945 and 1951 to 1955. He consistently warned Parliament of the perils of German expansionism and the foolishness of following a policy of appeasement. After losing office in 1945, he warned the world about Soviet expansionism in his 'Iron curtain' speech of 1946.

Sir Winston Churchill (1874–1965)

The roots of the debate lie in how the wartime disputes between the Grand Alliance are interpreted. **Traditional Soviet** historians emphasise the disagreements over the timing of a 'Second Front' in France. From June 1941 until June 1944 the USSR bore the brunt of the fighting against Germany, leading to horrendous Soviet suffering. From 1942 Stalin demanded that his allies should attack Hitler in the west. Stalin accused Churchill of breach of faith for not invading France. Churchill repeatedly assured Stalin that a second front in Europe would be opened up at the right time. However, he claimed that sufficient forces and supplies were vital, and that a premature attack would be suicidal. Thus, for two years Soviet suffering continued, and doubts in Stalin's mind, that the USSR was being used to drain the Nazi war machine so that his Grand Alliance partners could emerge victorious, seemed substantiated. Even in June 1944 Stalin was sceptical about '**D-Day**' actually occurring.

Traditional western historians saw Stalin's plan to dominate Europe after the war emerging in the actions of the Red Army in Eastern Europe. During 1944–5 Poland, Romania, Bulgaria and Yugoslavia were 'liberated' from the Nazis. Concerns over the future of these newly liberated states crystallised over Poland. Britain and France had gone to war in 1939 to protect Poland, but had failed to do so. Britain saw Poland as within its sphere of influence, as did Stalin. Poland had been the German invasion route to the USSR in 1941, thus control of Poland would give the USSR a buffer zone against future attack. Stalin, Roosevelt and Churchill (known as The Big Three) met at Teheran in November 1943 to discuss the Second Front and the boundaries of post-war Poland. Churchill suggested that the USSR should keep the areas of eastern Poland that they had seized in 1939, with Poland being compensated by receiving territory on her western border from Germany. By agreeing to the Nazi-Soviet Pact Polish boundary in the east, the western Allies had created a situation that no independent Polish government would accept. This meant that a 'puppet government' would have to be installed. Stalin had won the argument over Poland's future. **Revisionist** historians argued that the west's objections to Soviet policy towards Poland from 1945 were overstated in the light of the decisions taken at Teheran.

Events in Poland in 1944 have been used by traditional western historians to emphasise Stalin's evil intentions and actions. On 1 August 1944, the Polish Home Army rose up in Warsaw against the Germans. The Poles, who had links with their government in exile in London, were trying to liberate their capital before the Soviets arrived. The Red Army waited outside Warsaw for the Germans to

Traditional Soviet view: contemporary interpretation widely believed in the USSR, blaming the USA for the outbreak and development of the Cold War.

D-Day (1944): the start of the Allied invasion of Western Europe in the Second World War, when British and US troops landed on beaches in Normandy. After heavy fighting German forces evacuated most of France.

Traditional western view: contemporary interpretation widely believed in the west, blaming the USSR for the outbreak and development of the Cold War.

Revisionist view: interpretation that developed in the west in the 1960s and 1970s, blaming the USA for causing the Cold War.

crush the Poles. Although Stalin claimed that the strength of the German forces defending Warsaw meant that it was essential to wait and re-group the Red Army, the Soviet delay was interpreted in the west as hard-hearted cynicism. By January 1945 when Warsaw was 'liberated', Poland was in no position to determine its own future. Stalin's **Lublin Committee** were in government and the claims of the London Poles were ignored. In October 1944 Stalin and Churchill met in Moscow where they concluded what is known as the 'Percentages Agreement', concerning spheres of influence in post-war Europe. Post-revisionist historians have argued that both Stalin and Churchill were using the war for informal empire building.

Lublin Committee: the government of Poland installed by Stalin at the end of the Second World War.

The Yalta conference

The Big Three met at Yalta in the USSR in February 1945 to discuss the future of the soon-to-be-defeated Germany, while the Red Army was within forty miles of Berlin and U.S. and British troops were poised to cross the Rhine from the west.

The main disagreements at Yalta were over Poland. Churchill claimed that it was a matter of 'honour' for Britain that Poland would be 'free and sovereign' while Stalin outlined his concerns for Soviet security. Revisionists believe that the USA provoked the Cold

The Yalta conference

- To establish the United Nations

- To divide Germany and Berlin into four zones of occupation: French, US, UK and Soviet

- To divide Austria into zones of occupation

- Germany to pay reparations, primarily to the USSR; punishment of war criminals

- To instigate the principle of free elections in Poland and Soviet-occupied Eastern Europe

- Establishment of Korea's independence after a period of American and Soviet occupation

- The USSR agreed to declare war on Japan within three months

- The USSR agreed to a new government for Poland, based on their Lublin Committee

Post-revisionist view: interpretation that emerged in the 1970s, and was further developed at the end of the Cold War and the collapse of the USSR, arguing that no firm conclusion can be made concerning blame.

War by refusing to recognise legitimate Soviet interests in eastern Europe after the war. Stalin's concerns have been used by Soviet, revisionist, and **post-revisionist** historians to highlight the USSR's security needs.

The Potsdam conference

On 12 April 1945 Roosevelt died, and was succeeded by **Truman** who had little knowledge of world affairs. However, he quickly developed a 'Get Tough' policy towards the Soviets. On 30 April Hitler committed suicide, followed by Germany's surrender on 7 May. The war in Europe was over. In July, Stalin, Churchill and Truman met at Potsdam, outside Berlin. During the Conference, Labour defeated the Conservatives in the British election, so **Clement Attlee** replaced Churchill. Potsdam produced little new. The reparations agreement was firmed up, allowing each power the right to extract reparations from its own zone of Germany. Stalin also promised free elections in Poland. The conference ultimately papered over the widening cracks in the Grand Alliance. At Potsdam, it was revealed to Stalin that the USA had successfully exploded an atom bomb on 16 July. Revisionists have seen the dropping of the atomic bombs on Hiroshima and Nagasaki in August 1945, and the refusal of the USA to share the nuclear secret with the USSR, as heightening Stalin's legitimate security concerns. In 1948 the British physicist P. M. S. Blackett described the event as 'not so much the last military act of the Second World War as the first major operation of the Cold War'.

Truman (1884–1972)
A US politician, who was President from 1945–53. His decision to drop atomic bombs on Japan helped end the Second World War. He played a leading role in the establishment of the UN and of NATO. He toughened up US policy towards the USSR following the Second World War alliance.

The problem with Yalta and Potsdam was not an inability to find common ground but the failure to implement some decisions afterwards. In *Rise to Globalism: American Foreign Policy Since 1938* (1998), Stephen Ambrose outlined Roosevelt's initial feelings of triumph after Yalta, and how successive actions by Stalin shattered the calm: Stalin's refusal to reorganise the Polish government, his suppression of freedom of speech and the press in Poland, and his failure to hold the promised elections. These actions were central to the traditional western interpretation of the Cold War. Ambrose argued that these actions were repeated throughout Eastern Europe and claimed: 'The Soviet actions were high-handed, their suppressions brutal'.

Clement Attlee (1883–1967)
Britain's post-war Labour Prime Minister from 1945 to 1951. He was responsible for the Welfare State and ended his career as Leader of the Opposition 1951–5.

The Spread of Soviet control over Eastern Europe

The USSR was certainly in a strong position in Eastern Europe in 1945. Pro-communist coalition governments were in power and the promised elections were won by left-wing coalitions with a strongly communist flavour. Revisionist historians have stressed that it was the Red Army who had liberated these countries and how many people saw communism as something worth voting for. Truman thought that these elections were rigged, a view shared by traditional western historians. The communists swiftly merged with some of their coalition partners and ousted others. It would be naive to suggest there was no foul play. The USSR had good reasons for ensuring that the countries of Eastern Europe were in its camp whether for security or expansionist reasons.

By 1947 every Eastern European country except Czechoslovakia had a communist government modelled on the USSR's. Each country had influential Soviet 'advisers'. Policies like collectivisation and nationalisation were introduced, and leading opponents were purged. In the 1990s John Lewis Gaddis argued that the Cold War was 'an unavoidable consequence of Stalin's paranoia and an extension of the way he dealt with opposition within the USSR'.

The response of the west: the Truman Doctrine and Marshall Plan

By 1946 the Cold War 'battle lines' were drawn. In March 1946, Winston Churchill concluded: 'an Iron Curtain has descended across the continent', emphasising the plight of communist-dominated Eastern Europe. The containment of communism emerged clearly as US policy in 1947. In March, the announcement of the **Truman Doctrine**, by which the USA would 'support free peoples who are resisting attempted subjection by armed minorities or by outside pressure', directly implicated the USSR. Traditional western historians saw the Truman Doctrine as an essential defence mechanism against Soviet expansionism. Revisionist and Soviet historians viewed it as a provocative and threatening policy.

In June 1947 the USA introduced **Marshall Aid**. Traditional western historians saw this as an act of selfless generosity. Others have interpreted it as the economic muscles of the Truman Doctrine, combating the menace of communism by restoring prosperity to threatened nations. It was seen in the USSR as a cunning US plan to gain control over the global economy, a view supported by revisionist and left-wing historians. Unsurprisingly, Stalin rejected it on behalf of his 'eastern bloc'. In 1949 the USSR set up Comecon to coordinate the Eastern European economies and to provide some economic assistance.

Truman doctrine: The policy put forward by President Truman in a message to Congress in 1947 through which to contain the development of communism.

Marshall Aid: The proposal drawn up by the US secretary of state, George Marshall, offering US economic and financial help wherever needed to fight the chaos that followed the Second World War. To receive it a country had to give the USA access to its economic records and to open up their economy to US capitalism.

The Soviet domination of Eastern Europe by 1949.

Stalin's rejection of Marshall Aid led to an economic crisis and social discontent in Czechoslovakia by 1947. The Czech communists feared losing the 1948 elections. In response, the Communist Minister of the Interior began preparing a purge. In February 1948, eight non-communist Ministers resigned, thinking that this would immediately lead to elections. Instead they were simply replaced with communists. Elections were then held and the communists 'won' 237 of the 300 seats. This 'Czech Coup' brought the only 'free' state in Eastern Europe under Soviet control. Traditional western historians see this as further proof of Stalin's expansionist tendencies. By the time of the 'Czech Coup', Stalin had extended his Empire by gaining dominance over most of Eastern Europe. However, Stalin had also alienated the USSR from the USA and Great Britain.

The Berlin blockade and airlift

The division of Germany and Berlin at Potsdam was causing problems in 1948. By June 1948 the three western zones of Germany were united as Trizonia. Marshall Aid was pouring in and economic prosperity was returning. In stark contrast, the Soviet zone was facing poverty. Stalin was alarmed at how swiftly his former allies were rebuilding their defeated enemy. The traditional Soviet view was that the west was rebuilding Germany too quickly, in a manner that was directly threatening to the USSR. Berlin was a long way inside the Soviet zone of occupation. To reach their sectors of Berlin, the British, American and French had to use specially allocated routes. Western plans to introduce a new currency within their zones of Germany and Berlin was the catalyst for Stalin's Berlin blockade in 1948. Stalin aimed to starve west Berlin into the Soviet zone of Germany by cutting all routes between Berlin and western Germany. The response from Britain and the USA was the **Berlin Airlift**, which kept West Berlin supplied. Stalin could not have prevented their efforts without provoking a war. War was not an option at this time because in April 1949 the west had established **NATO**, and because the USA had previously demonstrated their awesome atomic power. During the blockade the USSR had no atomic weapons. Ironically, and to the horror of the west, this soon changed. The USSR tested their first atomic bomb in September 1949. The Cold War now posed a nuclear threat.

Berlin Airlift: President Truman and British Prime Minister Attlee's method for overcoming the land blockade in Berlin by keeping their part of Berlin supplied by air.

NATO (1949): The North Atlantic Treaty Organisation was a military alliance between the USA and Canada and most Western European nations.

Was Stalin's foreign policy successful?

If Stalin's main foreign policy aim was the defence and security of the USSR, then he had certainly achieved considerable success by the time of his death in 1953: safeguarding the USSR from conventional attack by his control over Poland; overcoming the USA's refusal to share their atomic secrets; and testing the USSR's own weapon of mass destruction. However, Stalin failed to prevent the German invasion of the USSR in 1941, which caused massive human loss. He also showed naivety in his signing of the Nazi-Soviet Pact in 1939, although it is difficult to see what other option he had. Despite this, the USSR played a huge role in the defeat of Germany from 1941–5. Stalin's industrial policies of the 1930s and the achievements of Five-Year plans contributed to this success. By 1945 the Red Army was probably the most powerful and effective fighting unit on the planet, although by 1949 his former allies in the Grand Alliance regarded the USSR as their sworn enemy.

If Stalin's main aim was expansionism, then the Soviet control of Poland, Bulgaria, Romania, Hungary, Czechoslovakia and East Germany by 1949 outlines his success. However, maintaining control over communist Yugoslavia and Albania within Eastern Europe, neither of which had a common border with the USSR, proved difficult. Stalin had also been unable to starve the west out of Berlin, or to prevent the unification of West Germany in 1949. The formation of NATO was also a significant block to further Soviet expansion.

By the time of his death, Stalin's USSR had been established as a global superpower. His legacy allowed the USSR to successfully challenge others through the nuclear arms race, and to successfully develop the Soviet Union's space programme, launching the world's first satellite, Sputnik. By 1961 the Russian, Yuri Gagarin, became the first man in space.

Was Stalin's foreign policy successful?

1. Read the following extract and answer the question.

    'The Germans invaded the USSR through Eastern Europe. The Germans were able to because governments hostile to the Soviet Union existed in those countries. As a result of the German invasion the USSR's loss of life was several times greater than that of Britain and the USA put together. Possibly in some quarters an inclination is felt to forget about these colossal sacrifices of the Soviet people, which secured the liberation of Europe from the Nazis. But the Soviet Union cannot forget about them. The USSR, anxious for its future safety, is trying to see to it that governments loyal in their attitude to the USSR should exist in these countries'.

    (Adapted from a speech by Stalin, 1946)

    Using information in the extract above, and from this chapter, discuss whether Stalin's actions in Eastern Europe from 1944 to 1948 were **only** undertaken for security reasons.

2. How valid is the view that Stalin's **main** foreign policy concern in the period 1924–53 was the defence and security of the USSR?

Was his economic policy effective?

What part did brutality play in his consolidation of power after 1929?

Was he no more than the 'Red Tsar'?

Framework of events

1928–9	Introduction of the first Five-Year Plan and 'collectivisation'
1932–3	Man made famine in Ukraine
1932	Suicide of Stalin's second wife, Nadezhda Alliluyeva
1933	Introduction of the second Five-Year Plan
1934	Assassination of Kirov
1935	Launch of the Stakhanovite campaign
1936	New Constitution introduced
1936–8	The Show Trials
1938	Introduction of the third Five-Year Plan
1940	Assassination of Leon Trotsky
1946	Introduction of the fourth Five-Year Plan
1951	Introduction of the fifth Five-Year Plan
1953	Stalin's death

Was Stalin's economic policy effective?

Why did Stalin abandon the NEP?

Stalin's dramatic change in economic policy has led to much debate. While some historians view this change as political opportunism – Stalin's chance to remove the rightists and seize power – others argue that it was a pragmatic response to the economic difficulties caused by the NEP. Low grain prices led to peasant unrest and a shortage of food in the towns. Thus Stalin introduced collectivisation and launched the Five-Year Plans. This committed the USSR to a planned economic policy, which aimed to match the economies of the advanced capitalist states. In November 1928, Stalin stated: 'We are going full steam ahead along the road to industrialisation'. The historian Michael Lynch, in his book *Stalin and Khrushchev, 1924–1964* (1990), argued that the Five-Year Plans were Stalin's 'attempt to establish a war economy'. In 1931, Stalin wrote that the USSR was years behind the west: 'we must make good this distance in ten years. Either we do it, or they crush us'. The Five-Year Plans gave the USSR the opportunity to build socialism while the west slumped into the **Great Depression**. Stalin's Five-Year Plans had great consequences for Soviet industry and agriculture.

The Great Depression (1929–34): a worldwide slump, starting with an agricultural recession followed by financial panic and collapse. This affected financial institutions and money markets across the world. The results were a decline in international sales and exports in industrialised countries.

Gosplan: The State Planning Commission established in 1921 responsible for setting targets for the Five-Year Plans.

How successfully did Stalin industrialise the USSR?

Historians such as E. H. Carr viewed the Five-Year Plans as the 'Second Revolution' and 'Stalin's Revolution'. **Gosplan** set targets for each plan, which industries were expected to meet.

The Five-Year Plans	Start	Finish
First Five-Year Plan	October 1928	December 1932
Second Five-Year Plan	January 1933	December 1937
Third Five-Year Plan	January 1938	June 1941 (interrupted by war)
Fourth Five-Year Plan	January 1946	December 1950
Fifth Five-Year Plan	January 1951	December 1955

Historians have had difficulty sorting out exaggerated Soviet claims from actual production figures. However, the table below shows the scale of Stalin's achievement:

	1928	1932	1937	1940 Before Barbarossa	1942 After Barbarossa	1945	1950
Electricity *(milliard kwths)*	5.05	20	80	90	29	43	91
Coal *(million tones)*	35.4	64.3	128	150	75	149	261
Oil *(million tones)*	11.7	21.4	26	26	22	19	38
Steel *(million tones)*	4.0	5.9	18	18	8	12	27

Gosplan targets were not always met but the economy was undeniably transformed by 1940, and re-built again after 1945. By 1940 steel production increased 450 per cent, coal production rose by over 500 per cent, oil production more than doubled and the generation of electricity soared. By 1940 the Gross National Product (GNP) had doubled.

The successes of the Five-Year Plans

- There was an economic growth rate of 5–6 per cent.

- New industrial regions to the east of the Urals were developed.

- Major new industrial centres, like **Magnitogorsk**, were created.

- Approximately 1500 power stations, factories and metalworking plants were built during the first plan alone.

- New industries such as machine-tools, synthetic rubber and aircraft were created.

The failures of the Five-Year Plans

- The need to meet targets meant quantity was more important than quality.

- Production figures were falsified to ensure targets were 'met'.

- The Belomor Canal, connecting the White Sea to the Baltic, was too shallow for the Soviet Navy's warships.

- Wages were lower in 1941 than 1928.

- Consumer goods were scarce because economic targets were aimed at expanding heavy industry.

- Training lagged behind technology.

How did the USSR achieve these industrial advances?

These results were achieved by:

Propaganda
Stalin portrayed the Five-Year Plans as the USSR's battleground with the slogan: 'There is no fortress the Bolsheviks cannot take'. The safety of the motherland was seen as depending on Soviet success. Each plan was announced complete one year ahead of schedule as a propaganda exercise to promote an image of achievement. Also, showpiece projects that demonstrated Soviet might, like the Moscow Metro, Magnitogorsk and the **Dnieprostroi Dam**, were given maximum publicity.

The expansion of Soviet industry and the threat of the gulag.

The Stakhanovite campaign

In 1931 Stalin abandoned level wages and replaced them with recognition and rewards for the most skilled and productive workers. The value of ordinary worker's wages almost halved between 1928 and 1940. In 1935 the **Stakhanovite campaign** was launched. Stakhanovite workers earned extra pay and privileges. Production output rose because workers competed to become 'Stakhanovites'.

Terror

Stakhanovite-style productivity was set as the norm. The sheer impossibility of meeting targets led to a culture of fear. The **gulags** provided the threat. Managers who failed to meet targets, or workers who accidentally broke machines, were accused and despatched to the gulags. Real reasons for failures were hidden behind accusations that 'kulaks' and 'Trotskyites' were deliberately sabotaging the Soviet dream. The unknown millions in the gulags provided the USSR with slave labour to carry out crucial tasks, such as gold mining, in the most inhospitable and remote regions. In *The Gulag Archipelago volume II* (1974), the Nobel Prize

Stakhanovite Campaign: named after Alexei Stakhanov, a Donbas coal-miner in the USSR, who cut 100 tons of coal in a single work-shift, 14 times his quota, in 1935.

Gulag: a forced labour camp. By the end of the 1930s, these were positioned all over the USSR.

Alexander Solzhenitsyn (b. 1918) A prominent Russian dissident who was arrested in 1945 while serving in the Red Army. After completing eight years in a gulag, he was exiled to Kazakhstan. After Stalin died, his successor, Krushchev, gave permission for the publication of his novel *One Day in the Life of Ivan Denisovich* in 1962 to encourage anti-Stalinist feeling. However, his succeeding books were banned as they contained dangerous criticisms of Soviet society. Despite this they found an enormous audience abroad. His vast work *The Gulag Archipelago* (1968) was published abroad and, during exile, he personally accepted his Nobel Prize.

winning author **Alexander Solzhenitsyn** described the brutality of the conditions in the gulags based on his own imprisonment and other prisoners' testimonies. One prisoner, Ivan Karpunich-Braven, described starving prisoners eating a dead horse 'which not only stank but was covered with flies and maggots'.

How successfully did Stalin develop agriculture within the USSR?

Agrarian: relating to land or agriculture.

Stalin's plan of transforming the USSR 'from an **agrarian** into an industrial' country had direct implications for the peasants: grain requisitioning and collectivisation.

Was collectivisation necessary?

In 1927 the USSR fixed the price of grain artificially low. Peasants responded to this by cutting back grain production and hoarding it. It wasn't worth selling because any money that they received wouldn't be enough to buy manufactured goods, which were scarce and expensive. The peasants' actions created an urban food shortages crisis. Historian Jerry Karcz criticised Stalin's regime for creating this crisis by fixing the price of grain so low. In contrast, historian Moshe Lewin believed that Stalin needed to act because grain collections were so low. As the supply of grain from the villages to the towns began to dwindle, Stalin acted decisively. In 1928, he alleged that wealthier kulak peasants were hoarding grain while the state was finding it difficult to feed the urban **proletariat**. In *Collected Works* (1955) Stalin stated that grain requisitioning would be sabotaged as long as kulaks existed. Between 1928 and 1930 a class war was waged against the kulaks. Poorer peasants were encouraged to point out kulaks who hoarded grain. These peasants were paid with 25 per cent of the grain seized.

Proletariat: the working class.

In January 1929, Stalin increased the tempo by calling for all grain producing areas to be collectivised by the autumn of 1930. At the Party Congress in December 1929 Stalin made a chilling demand: 'We must break the resistance of the Kulaks and deprive this class of its existence. We must eliminate the Kulaks as a class'. From 1929 to March 1930 there was a rush to collectivise farms. Approximately 60 per cent were collectivised. Peasant who objected were branded as kulaks and shot, or deported to the gulags. The Stalinist view, put forward by the Central Committee in 1939 in the *Short Course*, was that Stalin needed to save socialism by crushing the bourgeois, capitalist threat posed by the developing kulak class.

In 1976 James Millar and Alec Nove wrote *A debate on collectivisation: was Stalin really necessary?* (1964). Nove argued that in 1928 the conservative and backward peasantry reacted by eating more and working less, which made collectivisation necessary. Millar argued that the grain crisis of 1928 was a temporary problem that Stalin could have overcome by raising grain prices. Accordingly, there was no real crisis and no need for collectivisation. Nove argued that the USSR needed to industrialise rapidly for defence purposes, and that Stalin could only achieve rapid industrialisation through forcible collectivisation. Stalin needed to export huge quantities of agricultural produce to finance industrialisation. The liberal school of historians that developed in the west after the Second World War has been extremely critical of Stalin by emphasising the human cost of collectivisation.

Peasant resistance

Peasants resisted collectivisation to their best ability. Crops were burned and animals slaughtered in preference to handing them over. Mikhail Sholotov described the peasant reaction in his novel *Virgin Soil Upturned* (1955): 'Kill, it's not ours any more. Kill, you won't get meat on a collective farm.' By March 1930 Stalin faced peasant rebellion.

How did Stalin deal with the crisis in the countryside?

In March 1930 Stalin called a temporary halt to collectivisation to ensure that there would be a harvest in 1930. In his article *Dizzy With Success* (1930) in *Pravda*, Stalin stated that 'collective farms should not be imposed by force'. He claimed that party workers had been carried away in enforcing collectivisation. Peasants left the collectives across the USSR and the 1930 harvest was good. Putting collectivisation on hold got Stalin out of a difficult situation. As soon as the grain was harvested, collectivisation was re-enforced.

Some historians argue that Stalin had a 'cunning plan' in 1930. Norman Stone challenges the concept of Stalin as master-planner and suggests that he simply reacted to changing circumstances.

What were the outcomes in the countryside?

Results in the countryside were drastic. The number of cattle and pigs halved between 1928 and 1933, while the number of sheep and goats fell by two-thirds. Grain output fell dramatically from 83.5 to 69.5 million tonnes between 1930 and 1931. Extraordinarily both the state requisition of grain and its export abroad increased despite the poor harvest of 1931. The percentage of the grain harvest requisitioned rose from 26 per cent in 1930 to 33 per cent in 1931.

By 1932 the USSR was in the grip of a man-made famine. In 1932 a report from **Reuters** stated: 'The government's policy of collectivisation and the peasants' resistance to it have brought Russia to the worst catastrophe since the famine of 1921'. But instead of opening up the USSR to international aid, the Soviet authorities firmly denied such reports and imposed a five-year prison sentence for mentioning the famine. Some western visitors were fooled into denying its existence by visiting 'showcase' areas. Although the famine afflicted the Ukraine most severely, in *Russia Reported* (1934) Walter Durranty wrote: 'I can positively say that the harvest is splendid and all talk of a famine is ridiculous'.

Reuters: an international independent news agency.

Did the ends justify the means?

Stalin's main aim was to transform the Soviet Union into an industrial superpower, which he undoubtedly did. The Five-Year Plans led to a dramatic rise in industrial production, which enabled the USSR to emerge victorious in war against the Nazis in 1945. In *Behind The Urals (1942)* **John Scott** argued that Stalin's ruthless determination was 'responsible for the construction of Magnitogorsk and the entire Urals and Western Siberia industrial area'. However, Stalin's achievements had a severe human cost. Collectivisation had disastrous consequences for peasants, which Chris Ward summarises in *Stalin's Russia* (1999). He describes its incalculable impact: 'the whirlwind which swept across the countryside destroyed the way of life of the vast majority of the Soviet people'. Robert Conquest, in his book *Stalin: Breaker of Nations* (1991), has estimated that around seven million died in the famine, perhaps five million in the Ukraine. He describes the famine as a 'fight to the death against the peasantry – and, blended with it, against the Ukrainian nationality',

John Scott
An American volunteer who felt that Magnitogorsk was making history and wanted to be a part of it. He emigrated to the USSR and, in his book *Behind the Urals* (1942), documented his idealism and experiences.

Dekulakization:
Stalin's efforts to rid the
USSR of kulaks.

commenting that 'when Stalin was engaged in a fight to the death, there was always plenty of death to go around'. Similarly, nearly ten million people were forcibly removed from their villages under **dekulakization**. Trainloads were deported to the Siberian gulags. By 1939 approximately nineteen million people had left the countryside. However, Robert Service argues that Stalin gained 'a reservoir of terrified peasants' to act as cheap industrial workers. Stalin was also responsible for the terror and the gulags where prisoners lived and worked in atrocious conditions, and in which nearly twelve million people died.

In terms of agricultural output, the dramatic collapse in agricultural productivity in the early 1930s was not Stalin's aim. However, even as productivity fell, the grain procurements taken by the state did not. Many traditional historians agree that collectivisation enabled Stalin to gain the grain to feed the growing proletariat and to pay for imported industrial machinery. Collectivisation paved the way for industrial progress. However, revisionist historians like Aleksandr Barsov and J. R. Millar argue that money and resources had to be ploughed into the modernisation of agriculture, and that collectivisation made a 'negative contribution' to Stalin's plans. It is also argued that falling grain prices in the Great Depression meant that the USSR did not receive as much for their grain as Stalin would have hoped back in 1928.

Despite the undoubted industrial success of his economic policies, through his severe agricultural policy Stalin effectively caused the death of his second wife, Nadezhda Alliluyeva. In 1932, she learned of the terrible conditions and starvation in the Ukraine. Following an argument with Stalin, Nadezhda went home and killed herself. Her suicide note said that her reasons were political as well as personal. Stalin claimed that 'she left me as an enemy'. She was not the last person to suffer that fate.

What part did brutality play in Stalin's consolidation of power after 1929?

Following his transformation of the economy, Stalin set about revolutionising the Communist Party through a series of purges and Show Trials, which further consolidated his power.

The Murder of Sergei Kirov

In February 1934, at the Seventeenth Party Congress, defeated rivals like Zinoviev and Bukharin admitted past errors and praised

Sergei Kirov (1886–1934)
A member of the Bolsheviks before the 1917 revolutions. After 1917 Kirov worked his way up the ranks and became a member of the Central Committee in 1923. In 1926 he replaced Zinoviev as Party Secretary in Leningrad.

Stalin. Referring back to his power struggle against 'anti-Leninist groups', Stalin claimed that he had nothing left to prove or fight. However, some communists were speculating whether **Sergei Kirov**, the popular party boss in Leningrad, might be a more suitable General Secretary than Stalin. Kirov rejected these suggestions but made a monumental blunder by informing Stalin. At the Congress, Kirov received more votes than Stalin in the elections to the Central Committee. This led to the abolition of the post of General Secretary. Stalin and Kirov became 'Secretary of Equal Rank'. On 1 December 1934 Kirov was assassinated.

The traditional (totalitarian) interpretation is that Stalin was responsible for Kirov's death. The leading contemporary spokesman for this school is Robert Conquest who, in *Stalin and the Kirov Murder* (1989), accuses Stalin of ordering Kirov's murder. He is convinced that Stalin, motivated by what Chris Ward in *Stalin's Russia* (1999) has described as his 'morbid suspicion' and 'lust for power', was guilty. A different interpretation was provided by the revisionist historian John Arch Getty in *Origins of The Great Purges* (1985). Getty accepted Stalin's exploitation of Kirov's death for his own purposes, but doubted whether he actually ordered it. Revisionist historian R. W. Thurston has used evidence from the Soviet archives to explain why there are problems involved with the traditional view. In *Stalin: The Court of the Red Tsar* (2003), Simon Sebag Montefiore argues that 'it is surely naive to expect written evidence of the crime of the century'. He concludes that 'the mystery will never now be conclusively solved'.

Why did Stalin launch the purges?

In a brutal and cynical masterstroke Stalin used Kirov's death to launch the Great Purges to rid himself of any personal rival or enemy. Gripped by paranoia, Stalin saw rivals and enemies everywhere. Directly after Kirov's murder, Stalin passed the 'Law of 1 December 1934', which gave the **NKVD** special powers to execute people accused of terrorism without trial. Nikolaev, Kirov's assassin, was shot dead without trial, as were members of his family. Stalin's 'war on terrorism' began.

NKVD: the Soviet Security Service which included the secret police. Known until 1922 as the Checka, it was re-named OGPU (1923–4) and then the NKVD (1934–41).

Kirov was replaced in Leningrad by Zhdanov, and Khrushchev became Party Secretary in Moscow. Together they launched a witch-hunt to punish all those involved in the conspiracy to murder Kirov. Thousands of Kirov's supporters were dispatched to the gulags, accused of involvement in his death. In 1936 Stalin

LENIN'S GENERAL STAFF OF 1917
STALIN THE EXECUTIONER ALONE REMAINS

RYKOV Executed	BUKHARIN Executed	SVERDLOV Dead	STALIN Survivor	ZINOVIEV Executed	KAMENEV Executed	TROTSKY Assassinated	LENIN Dead
KOLLONTAI ?	SMILGA Executed	KRESTINSKY Executed	URITSKY Dead	NOGIN Dead	DZERZHINSKY Dead	BUBNOV Disappeared	SOKOLNIKOV Imprisoned
LOMOV ?	SHOMYAN Dead	BERZIN ?	MURANOV Disappeared	ARTEM Dead	STASSOVA Disappeared	MILIUTIN Disappeared	JOFFE Suicide

Part of a newspaper published by supporters of Trotsky in 1938, showing which of the Bolshevik leaders of 1917 had been purged.

reopened investigations into Kirov's murder. This paved the way for the Show Trials.

Who were Stalin's victims?

The Show Trials (1936–8) were used to eliminate real and imagined political rivals. In 1936 Kamenev and Zinoviev were arrested for 'opposition' and planning terrorist activities, most notably Kirov's murder. Their trial epitomised those that followed, with the accused confessing to made-up charges, being found guilty and executed. All the old Bolshevik heroes of 1917 – Stalin's rivals from the 1920s – were destroyed. Of the 139 members of the Central Committee in 1934, 98 were arrested and shot. 1108 out of the 1996 delegates to the Seventeenth Party Congress (at which more voted for Kirov than Stalin) also became victims.

The noose was extended way beyond the Communist Party. In July 1937 Yezhov produced a hit list of the 250 000 'most wanted'; these victims included artists, historians, scientists, writers and musicians. Historian Chris Ward has described it as an 'avalanche of monstrous charges, nightmarish allegations and random arrests'.

In the Military Trial of 1937 Marshall Tukhachevsky, the Commissar for Defence, was put on trial for treason along with an awesome array of military commanders. The victims included all 11

Deputy Commissars, 75 of the 80 members of the Supreme Military Council, and all of the USSR's eight Admirals. About half of the officers of the Red Army, approximately 35 000 people, were either imprisoned or executed. A key victim in 1938 was the former NKVD chief, Yagoda. In 1936 the bloodthirsty Yehzov replaced him after Stalin insisted that the NKVD was four years behind in its work. In 1939 Yezhov was blamed by Stalin for 'excessive zeal' and replaced by Beria. Yezhov became another victim, shot dead in February 1940.

By 1940 only Trotsky, in exile in Mexico, remained alive. He too had to die. Stalin's agent was sent to Mexico, where on 20 August 1940 he murdered Trotsky, marking the end of Stalin's rivals.

Was Stalin totally responsible for the Purges?

Totalitarian (Intentionalist) historians believe that because Stalin wielded total power the instructions must have come from the top. In *The Great Terror: A Reassessment* (1990), Robert Conquest endorses this interpretation, arguing that Stalin ordered the purges to consolidate his power. The opening up of the Soviet archives after the collapse of communism has lent weight to this traditional view. However, the revisionist school argue that there was a bottom-up dimension to the purges as well as the traditional top-down view. They cite Stalin's sacking of Yezhov for 'excessive zeal' as evidence that leaders of the NKVD acted on their own initiative. Also, many colleagues, neighbours and family members denounced victims. In 1932, 13-year old Pavlik Morozov denounced his own father. In 1933, the poet Osip Mandelstam wrote a poem implying that 'every killing is a treat' for Stalin. Mandelstam recited it to several 'friends' who informed on him. Mandelstam died in a labour camp in 1938.

A leading exponent of the revisionist school is J. Arch Getty who wrote *The Origins Of The Great Purges* in 1985. In his book *Koba The Dread,* Martin Amis attacked Getty by stating that if he continues 'revising at his current rate, he will eventually be telling us that only two people died in the Great Terror, and that one very rich peasant was slightly hurt during collectivisation'. However, In *The Road To Terror: Stalin and the Self-Destruction of the Bolsheviks* (1999), written with O.V. Naumov, Getty insists that the terror was not 'the culmination of a well-prepared and long-standing master-design', but accepts that 'Stalin's guilt for the terror was never in question. We can now see his finger marks all over the archives'.

Did the purges of the 1930s strengthen Stalin's position?

By the end of the 1930s Stalin had effectively wiped out all traces of opposition against his political position. Old Russian revolutionaries had been removed and a younger generation of officials had replaced them. However, it is arguable that the purges severely undermined Stalin's regime. His execution of so many military officers severely weakened the Red Army command structure whilst the world was poised on the brink of war.

Was Stalin no more than a 'Red Tsar'?

Stalin has often been described as the 'Red Tsar'. In *Russia 1881–1924: Reaction and Revolutions* (1992) Michael Lynch compared government before and after 1917. He concluded that 'it was the replacement of one form of state authoritarianism by another'. In *Stalin in Power: The Revolution from Above* (1992), Robert Tucker claims that Stalin was just one in a long line of Russian leaders who forced change from above (see **Landmark Study**, below) The Tsars upheld **autocracy**; Lenin and Stalin imposed dictatorship. Stalin was much more effective at eradicating opposition than most Tsars. There are clear elements of continuity between Stalin's USSR and the past, but there are also significant areas of change. Was Stalin a 'Red Tsar' – simply re-imposing past values on the present – or did he revolutionise Russian society?

Autocracy: rule by one person with complete power.

Was there a social revolution?

The extent to which there was a social revolution is debated. The traditional (totalitarian) view presents Soviet society as a passive, pliable object moulded by Stalin. Revisionists like Geoffrey

---

Landmark Study | The book that changed people's views

Robert C. Tucker, *Stalin in Power: The Revolution from Above, 1929–1941*, (W. W. Norton & Co., 1992)

This book formed the second volume of Tucker's biography of Stalin. The first was: *Stalin as Revolutionary 1879–1929.* Tucker is an American historian who portrays Stalin as a member of the radical right of the Communist Party. He identifies continuity between Stalin's revolution from above with previous periods of great political, social and economic change during the Tsarist period. In this sense Stalin is portrayed as continuing Russian tradition rather than breaking with the past. To Robert Tucker Stalin plunged the USSR into a decade long revolution from above from 1929. The coercing of 24 million peasant families into collective farms, the forced and rapid industrialisation of the USSR, and the liquidation of political and military opponents were seen as a planned response to the USSR position by Stalin as autocrat.

Hosking in *A History of the Soviet Union* (1985) challenge the view that Stalin shaped all artistic, scientific and cultural policy. Many historians focus on the way in which policies changed through time. In *The Great Retreat* (1946) Nicholas Timasheff suggested that the USSR experienced two periods of radical socialist experimentation: one post-1917, and a second as collectivisation and the Five-Year Plans were introduced. The revisionist historian Sheila Fitzpatrick, in *Cultural Revolution in Russia* (1978), describes the period from 1928 to 1931 as the USSR's cultural revolution. She emphasises that it emerged from below, rather than being imposed from above. In 1931, Stalin called a halt to the cultural revolution and began to re-impose more traditional values. Timasheff describes the period from 1934 as 'the Great Retreat' because all communist experiment was abandoned.

Soviet schooling demonstrates the impact of these changes. After the October Revolution teachers were reduced in status and forbidden to discipline pupils. In the cultural revolution testing and homework were attacked. After 1934 examinations, homework, school uniform and discipline were all re-instated. Education became a tool for indoctrination. In the 1930s schoolchildren were instructed to paste pieces of paper over disgraced party leaders in their textbooks. The purged old Bolsheviks became the 'disappeared'.

The return to a more traditional schooling policy was mirrored in other aspects of Soviet life. After 1917 divorce was made very easy to obtain and abortions were legalised. Stalin re-introduced traditional family values in 1936. Divorce was made much more difficult. Abortion, homosexuality and prostitution were banned. Mothers with more than six children were rewarded. Moshe Lewin has described these measures as 'classical social conservatism'.

Stalin introduced a new constitution in 1936, which gave the Soviet Union a democratic facade. Everyone over 18 gained the vote and elections were held every four years by secret ballot. However, only Communist Party candidates could stand. The constitution also listed human rights, including freedom of speech and freedom from arrest without trial, which would have been almost unrecognisable for the average Soviet citizen.

Under Stalin, the USSR was transformed from an overwhelmingly agricultural society to an increasingly industrial and urban society. Cities and towns expanded rapidly. Many young Soviets worked with fanatical idealism, but many more Soviets worked in the forced labour camps or gulags as slaves. The vastly expanded urban proletariat lived in grim conditions of violence and crime.

Doctored pictures show the 'disappearance' of Trotsky and Kamenev after their removal from government.

Food shortages, a lack of consumer products and harsh factory discipline made Soviet cities bleak places.

After 1917, the Bolsheviks introduced compulsory adult literacy classes. By 1939, 94 per cent of town-dwellers were literate and there was a free health service. These were significant changes. Despite Stalin's return to social conservatism, the role of women changed. In towns women worked alongside men, doing work that was unthinkable in most other countries at that time. This trend escalated out of necessity during the Second World War.

Under the Tsars, the Orthodox Church had been a pillar of the system. Religious indoctrination taught the peasants loyalty to the Tsar. Under communism religion was persecuted. The 'League of the Godless' developed an anti-religious school curriculum. After 1928 churches were closed and converted to other uses. Priests were put in prison or executed. In 1929 Sunday was abolished as a day of rest, probably to ensure continuous production. The communists also attacked Islam. The cult of the individual led to the deification of the dead Lenin and the living Stalin. The worship of God was replaced with the cult of the leader. Whether the peoples' religious faith was really eradicated is doubtful. Stalin may have changed the USSR more on the outside than he changed Soviet people on the inside.

In what ways did Stalinism represent a continuity with the past?

Many historians argue that problems such as the size of the USSR, the need to modernise and a desire to impose dictatorship, led Stalin to adopt policies that displayed a distinct continuity with past Russian regimes. The table below demonstrates the significant areas of continuity that existed between Stalin's USSR and Russia's past. However, it can certainly be argued that there were significant differences of scale, for example in Stalin's use of terror.

Area of Comparison	Tsarist Russia	Lenin's Russia	Stalin's Russia
Government	■ Autocratic	■ Dictatorial	■ Dictatorial
Repression & Secret Police	■ The Okhrana	■ The Cheka ■ The 'Red Terror'	■ The OGPU / NKVD ■ The Purges and Show Trials
Peasants	■ Oppressed ■ Squeezed by state to finance industrialisation ■ Encouraged to become Kulaks under Stolypin ■ Famine 1891	■ Oppressed ■ Squeezed by state under War Communism ■ Encouraged to become Kulaks under NEP	■ Oppressed ■ Squeezed by state to finance industrialisation under Collectivisation ■ Famine 1932–3
Minority races	■ Russification ■ Anti-Semitism	■ Famine 1921 ■ Semi-independent during Civil War ■ Russification enforced by Stalin from 1921 in his role of Commissar for Nationalities.	■ Russification ■ Anti-Semitism

Animal Farm: written in 1945 by George Orwell. It is a satire on the Russian Revolution in which animals on a farm overthrow their cruel farmer. This book had a tremendous impact on the way in which people viewed Stalin.

Was Stalinism Leninism?

In *Animal Farm* (1945) George Orwell, the British novelist and writer, blamed Stalin for all the problems of the USSR. This view was given a major boost in 1956 when Khrushchev astonished the world by delivering his 'secret speech' to the Twentieth Party Congress. Khrushchev read out Lenin's Political Testament and catalogued Stalin's crimes and failings. Stalin was guilty of 'flagrant abuses of power', including the terror and the purges. Khrushchev appeared to have revealed the USSR's inner secrets to point the finger of guilt at Stalin. He stated that 'Lenin used severe methods only in the most necessary cases. Stalin used extreme methods and mass repressions when the revolution was victorious. In this lies the whole tragedy'. In 1937, before his murder, Trotsky wrote his *History of the Russian Revolution*. He stated: 'the present purge draws between Bolshevism and Stalinism a whole river of blood'. In 1960, in *The Communist Party of the Soviet Union,* Leonard Schapiro concluded that 'Stalin's rule differed from Lenin's in its greater degree of totalitarian despotism' while in 1977 in *The Political Biography of Stalin*, Roy Medvedev argued that 'in most respects there is no continuity between Stalinism and Leninism'.

Right-wing western historians have drawn little distinction between Lenin and Stalin. However the school of thought suggesting that Stalin simply continued Lenin's policies has grown significantly since the 1980s. The openness encouraged under **glasnost** in the 1980s led to a frank re-evaluation of Lenin. This trend has escalated since the collapse of the USSR and the further opening of the Soviet archives. A view of Lenin as cynical dictator has emerged. Some historians have switched camps. In 1988 the Soviet historian, Dmitri Volkgonov, argued that Lenin's failure to remove Stalin in 1922–3 was the critical moment in the history of the USSR. In 1994 he concluded that Lenin was the chief architect of the terror state.

Lenin ruled dictatorially. He banned factions within the Communist Party and established the Cheka and the 'Red Terror'. The issue is was he a dictator by choice or circumstance? It is easy to argue that Lenin had to pursue practical policies simply to enable his regime to survive. However, those who believe Lenin chose to be a dictator make a persuasive case. In 1994, in *Russia Under the Bolshevik Regime*, Richard Pipes argued that 'every ingredient of what has become known as Stalinism save one – murdering fellow communists – he [Stalin] learned from Lenin', including 'collectivisation and mass terror'.

There may be some middle ground. In 1997 Robert Service, in *A History of Twentieth Century Russia*, wrote that 'it is hard to imagine Lenin carrying out a terror upon his own party. Lenin would have been horrified by the scale and methods of the Great Terror'. In *A People's Tragedy: The Russian Revolution 1891–1924* (1997) Orlando Figes agreed that the basic building blocks of Stalinism were put in place by Lenin, but feels that there were

Glasnost: Russian for 'openess', it was the Soviet policy, introduced in 1985, of allowing more freedom of press and speech, and showing greater concern for the right of the individual.

'fundamental differences between Lenin's regime and that of Stalin.' There are certainly strong elements of continuity between Stalinism and Leninism but clear differences of scale – certainly in relation to Stalin's use of terror. Perhaps Stalinism simply took Leninism to its unnatural extremes.

 How successful were Stalin's domestic policies?

1. Read the following extract and answer the question.

   'The Second World War was Stalin's victory. It could not have been won without his industrialisation campaign. Collectivisation contributed to victory, enabling the government to stockpile food and raw materials. Collectivisation gave the peasants their first training in the use of tractors. It had been the peasants' preparatory school for mechanised warfare'

   (Adapted from Ian Grey, *Stalin, Man of History*, Weidenfeld & Nicholson, 1979)

   Using information in the extract above, and from this chapter, discuss whether Stalin's achievements can justify his methods.

2. To what extent was Stalin nothing more than a brutal dictator?

Stalin: an assessment

Stalin's period in power began in the post-revolutionary period. When he died, the USSR was a global superpower, dominating much of Eastern Europe and challenging the USA through the Cold War.

How did Stalin become leader of the USSR?

Stalin gained immense political authority and influence under Lenin, particularly as General Secretary from 1922. He used his dominance over the political structures of the Communist Party extremely effectively. A combination of Stalin's cunning and the foolish mistakes of his rivals enabled him to win supreme power. Stalin also showed real political skill in manipulating the ideological economic debate to his own advantage.

Stalin's foreign policy: defensive or expansionist?

From 1924 Stalin realised that the expansion of world communism was impractical. Seeking security for the USSR became a dominant theme after Hitler became leader of Germany. Stalin tried to achieve this through collective security, but in 1939 sought salvation in the Nazi-Soviet Pact. From 1941 Stalin and the USSR were engaged in a titanic struggle for survival against Nazi Germany. By 1945 the USSR emerged victorious. After 1945, Stalin's takeover of Eastern Europe is central to the Cold War debate. Some historians believe that Stalin's actions were aimed at defending the USSR from future attack while others see expansionist goals in them.

Stalin's domestic policy: brutal but effective?

Stalin's effectiveness in terms of modernising the USSR is debateable. The Five-Year Plans introduced rapid industrialisation. Victory in the Second World War may justify their effectiveness. However, collectivisation left the USSR with an inefficient agricultural system.

Stalin's regime was certainly brutal, demonstrated by the gulags, de-kulakization, and the purges. Yet his brutality was effective, enabling him to rule supreme. However, when Stalin died, the USSR was left paralysed with fear and suspicion.

Further reading

Text specifically designed for students

Conquest, R. *Stalin Breaker of Nations* (Phoenix Giant 1991)
Corin, C and Fiehn, T. *Communist Russia Under Lenin and Stalin* (John Murray, 2002)
Isaacs, J and Downing, T. *Cold War* (Bantam Press 1998)
Lynch, M. *Stalin and Khrushchev: The USSR, 1924–1964* (Hodder & Stoughton, 1990)
Orwell, G. *Animal Farm* (Penguin Books, 1989)
Oxley, P. *Russia 1855–1991 From Tsars to Commissars* (Oxford University Press, 2001)
Phillips, S. Stalinist Russia (Heinemann, 2000)

Texts for more advanced study

Bullock, A. *Hilter and Stalin: Parallel Lives* (HarperCollins Publishers, 1998) outlines the source of Stalin's foreign policy.
Carr, E. H. *A history of Soviet Russia* (Macmillan, 1978) is a detailed work covering the rise of the Bolsheviks.
Mawdsley, E. *The Stalin Years* (Manchester University Press, 2003) covers Stalin's domestic policies thoroughly.
Montefiore, S. S. *Stalin: The Court of the Red Tsar* (Weidenfeld & Nicholson, 2003) offers an excellent insight into Stalin's personal life and his inner circle.
Tucker, R. *Stalin as Revolutionary 1879–1929: A Study in History and Personality* (Chatto & Windus, 1974) clearly outlines Stalin's rise to power.
Tucker, R. *Stalin in Power: The Revolution from Above 1929–1941* (W. W. Norton & Co., 1992) identifies the continuities between Stalin and previous Russian leaders.
Ward, C. *Stalin's Russia, 2nd Edition* (Arnold, 1999) is particularly good on the historical debates concerning Stalin's foreign policy.

Index